11/11/05

iX

EVALUATING
LIBRARY
STAFF

A Performance
Appraisal System

Patricia Belcastro

American Library Association
Chicago and London
1998

Project editor: Louise D. Howe

Cover by Richmond Jones

Printed on 50-pound White Offset, a pH-neutral stock, and bound in 10-point coated cover stock by McNaughton & Gunn

The paper used in this publication meets the minimum requirements of American National Standard for Information Sciences—Permanence of Paper for Printed Library Materials, ANSI Z39.48-1992.

Library of Congress Cataloging-in-Publication Data

Belcastro, Patricia.
    Evaluating library staff : a performance appraisal system / Patricia Belcastro.
      p.   cm.
    Includes index.
    ISBN 0-8389-0731-8
    1. Library employees—Rating of—United States.   I. Title.
Z682.28.B45   1998
023′ .9—dc21   97-32669

Printed in the United States of America.

02 01 00 99   5 4 3 2

CONTENTS

ACKNOWLEDGMENTS

The performance appraisal system described in this book would not have been possible without the support of the staff, administration, and the Board of Trustees of Rocky River Public Library, Rocky River, Ohio. Through an intensive year-long process, a dedicated group of library supervisors worked together to create, develop, and implement an evaluation system that answered the staff's request to be evaluated fairly on what they do daily. This supervisory team included Patricia Belcastro, Connie Fillinger, Michael G. Garrison, Elaine Hoke, Fran Homa, Sandra Kuban, Sarah McAllister, Sue Padavick, Randy Page, Ann Richey, and Bev Robertson. Without their efforts—and the continued involvement of other supervisors and staff each year—this book would not have been written.

Examples of performance behaviors used throughout the book are based upon composites of real-life situations and in no way reflect the actions of specific individuals.

Introduction

Evaluating Quality
of Performance

Continuous improvement has become a key phrase for all types of organizations, from for-profit companies to service providers. The goal of continuous improvement is to ensure the highest quality possible. Judging quality in manufactured gadgets, however, differs from evaluating the quality of service provided in a library or an information service center, when service performance—not a gadget—is the product. How to evaluate quality of performance in such an intense service setting as a library is the purpose of this how-to manual. The method described is a complete system for performance appraisal in libraries. The actual performance appraisal documents (with the accompanying guidelines) included in this book permit library managers to use the system as is, or, if preferred, easily adapt the performance appraisal documents to their specific needs.

Background: Evaluate Us for What We Do Daily

This performance appraisal system was developed by one library's supervisors and administration in response to the staff's overwhelming cry to "evaluate us for what we do daily." The performance standards in this appraisal system are directly related to behaviors that ensure the delivery of high quality service every day. The staff asked to be evaluated on their performance in their daily interactions with each other and the public they serve. The library's supervisors responded by spending twelve months devising standards and guidelines based on years of actual experience in providing service.

The supervisors, as a team, spent an entire year first discussing what the library expected of its staff in a strong service environment, and then writing, debating, and rewriting standards of performance based on those expectations. All areas of service—clerical, custodial, paraprofessional, and professional—were represented in the often heated debate.

Once the performance system was agreed upon by the supervisors, it was reviewed by all staff and approved by the board of trustees, the library's governing body. Even after implementation, it continues to be revised annually based on comments from both staff and supervisors. At this annual revision, new standards are added. For example, a standard on using technology was added two years after the original standards were written to reflect the rapid expansion of technology in library-wide service. This performance appraisal system is a "living" document that reflects the changing demands staff encounter in an evolving service setting.

The Key Is Communicating Expectations

The evaluation process is designed to measure fairly the quality of performance of library employees, including clerical, custodial, paraprofessional, and professional staff. This method is based on the expectations of the employer (the library), with those expectations clearly articulated through a Code of Service, job descriptions, and, finally, a performance appraisal document with guidelines. The key to the successful implementation of this performance appraisal system is the managers' ability to communicate to the staff their expectations for performance. For an employee to perceive any evaluation as fair, the employer must first clearly state what is expected of the employee—and then measure the meeting of (or noncompliance with) those expectations (standards of performance) in the most objective manner possible.

The Purpose of the Appraisal

The purpose of this complete performance appraisal system is first, to maintain a level of service consistent with the library's Code of Service or statement of its role or vision; second, to recognize those employees who exceed the expectations; and finally, but most important, to coach the employees who have not performed up to the expectations to improve to at least the "meets standards" level. A major benefit of this system is that it provides accountability to the public the library serves. The customers, patrons, students, faculty, or business people being served can be assured that the library is evaluating its staff on the criteria most important to those being served.

Using this system, both supervisor and employee are on the same path. Both understand the purpose of the evaluation. And since one of the appraisal process's primary functions is to provide the opportunity for improvement in performance, the appraisal is not a one-time checklist evaluation, but rather an *ongoing assessment* of on-the-job performance.

This performance appraisal system is not intended to replace any personnel policies or disciplinary procedures of the library. Codified personnel policies ensure that conditions of employment, compensation, benefits, and similar library-wide administrative actions are applied evenly and fairly. A discipline policy, with guidelines for verbal and written warnings, suspensions, and discharge, provides a uniform response from supervisors and managers to job-related offenses. This performance appraisal system should *complement* the values of the organization already set forth in those documents.

Focus Is on the Practical

This appraisal system's focus is on evaluating performance as it relates to the delivery of quality service. Emphasis is on the practical rather than the theoretical. The standards by which the employee is being judged are relevant first, to providing service, and second, to the actual job position. The Code of Service, job descriptions, and especially the appraisal document and its guidelines are intricately tied to actual performance in a library setting.

As a guide for the user of this manual, case studies (of fictitious employees, based on actual situations) with completed performance appraisal documents—linked to various jobs within the library—demonstrate in real-life situations how this system is used to measure quality of performance.

Use of the Appraisal System

The intended audience for this how-to manual is any library that does not presently have an effective and fair performance appraisal system or one whose managers are looking at ways to change the current evaluative process. Medium to small libraries—whether academic, special, or public—with no human resource person or department are welcome to tailor this "ready-made" system to their specific needs.

All of the documents described in this manual are included in the appendixes. Appendix A contains the Code of Service of Rocky River Public Library. Appendix B contains the Standards of Performance Guidelines described in Chapter 5 and Appendix C contains the Supervisory Procedures for Conducting a Performance Evaluation. The Performance Appraisal Document itself is Appendix D and the Tabulation Sheet is Appendix E. These documents may be reproduced for use in your library or information center.

For this system to be truly effective, it must be reviewed by staff—those who will be doing the evaluations and those who will be evaluated—to ensure that supervisors and staff agree that the standards accurately reflect the level of service expected at their library. Group discussions during which staff members can voice their interpretations of the standards and accompanying guidelines are very useful for fine-tuning the wording to prevent misunderstandings. Following this format of review, adjustments are made to reflect closely the performance expected at a particular library.

Accountability

As tax dollars stabilize or diminish and downsizing continues as a viable option, the demand for accountability for good library service increases. A performance appraisal system based on expectations of quality service not only provides that accountability to the library's clients, customers, or patrons, but also reinforces the value of the service the library provides. Most important, it is fair to the person being evaluated.

Many library managers avoid performance appraisal either from lack of time to develop a workable system or from fear of evaluating performance subjectively rather than objectively. This book is intended for them.

1

Expectations for Quality Service

In any service organization, there are expectations. The person being served—whether customer, patron, client, student, faculty, or business person—has his or her own perspective when interacting with the library's staff. That perspective is often based on the individual's unique view of what constitutes quality service, his or her past experiences, the work or personal style of the individual, or the particular circumstances surrounding the contact (e.g., the person being served is rushed, impatient, or angry because of something that happened just prior to any contact with a library employee).

What Is Quality Service?

The staff of a service provider such as a library or information center also have very individual perceptions of what comprises "quality" service. One staff member may think that just being available at a service desk (arriving when scheduled and remaining at the desk until his or her shift is up) means that he or she is ready to serve, thus providing the expected quality of service. Another staff member may be more proactive, actually rising when someone approaches the desk or perhaps not even remaining at the desk, but wandering the stacks looking for people needing assistance. Which staff member is providing quality service?

Well, it depends. What are the "values" of the library for which these people are working? Is it important for the library's mission to have a staff member readily available at a specific service point to answer a phone, e-mail, or in-person request? Perhaps, for a special library, that instant response is vital. Is it important for the library's mission to have a staff member exhibit friendly, welcoming behavior? Perhaps in a community or public library, yes. However, in some communities, people entering a library may not want a service provider leaping up and instantly accosting them to offer help. They may feel put on the spot or rushed to make a decision when all they want to do is browse. Community expectations are key.

Before any manager can fairly evaluate an employee, that manager must communicate to the employee the expectations for quality service. An employee has the essential right to know the standards on which he or she is being judged—before any evaluation process begins. Those standards of performance, or expectations of service, are based on the values of the organization.

What Are the Values of the Organization?

What are the values of the organization? Basically, how effectively a library meets the needs of its users is what makes that library or information center essential to its community of users. Once staff understand the needs and the expectations of the library's users, they can articulate clearly the library's role or mission. From the role and mission come the values of the library. For example, if it is determined that a library's clientele wants friendly, but not overly solicitous, service, its values will include a welcoming, but not proactive ("jumping up" or approaching people) service environment. From that particular value, it is possible to describe specific behaviors that reinforce friendly service. These desired behaviors become part of the standards of performance for the employees.

Standards Express the Library's Expectations

Since the standards of *performance* are developed from an understanding of the library's role or mission, the values implicit in the role or mission provide the foundation for fair standards of *evaluation*. They are based on the perceived expectations of the community as a whole. An employee interacting with a client or patron then uses behaviors that will effectively fulfill the library's stated mission.

If it has been determined that a library's community of users wants to be welcomed, the library's standards should reflect that specific expectation. For example, one standard of performance could be "makes eye contact, greets others sincerely, and speaks in a friendly manner." A different standard (based on the level of welcoming the library has determined its users want) could be "advances to greet the customer, escorts him or her to the desired area in a friendly manner." In another library, an appearance of overeagerness or "pushiness" may be discouraged. Here, the standard of performance for this value of the organization might be "responds to the client in a friendly manner when the client indicates that he or she needs help." An employee knows that his or her employer (the library or organization) expects all staff to welcome a user or client. How that welcoming is accomplished is what must be stated clearly in the standard of performance.

Behaviors Must Be Measurable

Whatever the standard of performance, it is based on behaviors that can be measured, not on attitudes that may be interpreted subjectively. The phrase "is friendly" is a subjective expression reflecting someone's perception of an attitude. However, "speaks in a friendly manner" is an act or a way of conducting oneself. It is observable and can be documented by noting the reactions which that particular manner evokes from the recipient. Every employee, whatever his or her temperament, is capable of speaking in a friendly manner and can be fairly evaluated according to his or her acts or behaviors.

2

Code of Service

How are a library's values communicated to its employees and the public it serves? One way is to condense its role or mission (whether written or unwritten) into succinct, broad statements of performance that are easily understood not only by the library's staff, but also by its users. The Code of Service is a snapshot of the values of the library or information center. A patron, client, student, or user reading the Code has an immediate impression of what is considered vital to that particular library's mission—service, education, research, a warehouse of information, a popular collection—and how the staff will carry that out.

The Foundation

A Code of Service is the foundation upon which the performance appraisal system is based. Such a document is approved by the policy-making board of the organization and applies to all staff within the organization. Its broad performance statements represent the philosophy or values of the organization. From it flow the standards of performance, which describe even more specifically the expected performance. The specific standards of performance based on the Code further elaborate the behaviors which confirm that value or philosophy. Any employee reading the standards of performance knows exactly what performance is expected of him or her to fulfill the library's mission.

If a library's mission in an academic setting is "to provide information and services to faculty and students," then its Code of Service simply and clearly states how that mission is to be accomplished. Elements could include such statements as, "the user of State College Library, whether faculty or student, is entitled to a courteous, timely response" and "the State College Library staff is committed to providing students up-to-date and relevant instruction on how to use the library." A student reading this college library's Code knows that he or she can expect timely service and relevant instruction on how to use the library's collections.

The Code of a special library might state that "the information center will meet the business research needs of the individual by using all available resources both within and outside the company." This statement implies that the philosophy of the information center is to go to great lengths to answer a business research need.

Rocky River Public Library states its values in the following Code of Service:

CODE OF SERVICE
Rocky River Public Library

- The library public is entitled to easily accessible library collections in a safe, clean, organized, and appropriate environment staffed with friendly, courteous people.

- Each member of the library public is to be welcomed, fairly and courteously, without discrimination.

- Service to the public takes precedence over the library's internal paperwork and internal communications.

- Information given to the library public will be based on verifiable, current sources, clearly communicated, and given in a timely manner.

Through this Code, both the library's staff and the public it serves know that the values of Rocky River Public Library include a welcoming and courteous environment, accessible collections, and an emphasis on service above all else. An employee understands that service to the patron is at the center of the library's role.

The Code's Effectiveness

A Code of Service is most effective when its statements have been thoroughly discussed, debated, and distilled into a succinct form by the staff to whom the code applies. The people who will be implementing the Code (e.g., supervisors or managers) should be directly involved in its development. Such involvement acknowledges various perspectives on the library's role or mission, generates a Code that accurately reflects the delivery of service, and provides a framework for the more difficult task of defining standards that support the Code. Once a Code has been written, it is approved by the governing board or executive of the library. That seal of approval represents full support of the performance standards that sustain the values expressed in the Code.

Your Code of Service is the foundation upon which the performance appraisal system is built. Make it a statement you can be proud of.

From the Code to the Standards

You have examined what makes your library or information center effective in serving its community of users. From that review you have determined the library's role and the values that support that role. From that role or mission you have written the broad statements that support the library's values and apply to all staff in your library. These statements comprise your library's philosophy or Code of Service.

Now it is time to translate the generalities of that Code into the specific standards of performance expected of your employees. The standards of performance flow from the Code and clearly articulate the specific behaviors that support the values expressed in the code. Look at your Code and ask yourself: What *behaviors* support this philosophy of service?

The Standards As Actions or Behaviors

The standards are a written expression of the expectations of the library for quality service. They are written as actions or behaviors. Behaviors can be modified, but attitudes usually cannot. For example, the standard, "makes eye contact, greets others sincerely, and speaks in a friendly manner," is a set of behaviors, while "is pleasant and cheerful" is an attitude. Even an employee who is not a normally cheerful person is capable of making eye contact and greeting others sincerely. "Is friendly" is an attitude or personality trait, but "speaks in a friendly manner" is a behavior that can be learned, if necessary. These behaviors—makes eye contact, greets others sincerely, and speaks in a friendly manner—are actions that can be evaluated objectively based on the reactions of others to the employee's words or manner.

Initially, when considering what behaviors support your library's code or values, it is helpful to think of behaviors that are *not* desirable. Then the desired behavior is strikingly evident. It is also helpful to think of behaviors outside of the library setting that reinforce the type of service the library desires. Quality service, whatever the environment in which it is delivered, has common behavioral elements.

The Standards Express the Quality Service Desired

The degree of quality service desired is expressed in the standards of performance. Once behaviors that represent quality service have been identified, these behaviors can be translated into clear standards for employees. Each employee knows what is expected of his or her perfmance in this service environment. For example, let's look again at the Code of Service for Rocky River Public Library (RRPL).

CODE OF SERVICE
Rocky River Public Library

- The library public is entitled to easily accessible library collections in a safe, clean, organized, and appropriate environment staffed with friendly, courteous people.

- Each member of the library public is to be welcomed, fairly and courteously, without discrimination.

- Service to the public takes precedence over the library's internal paperwork and internal communications.

- Information given to the library public will be based on verifiable, current sources, clearly communicated, and given in a timely manner.

The Code indicates that this particular library strives to be a warm, welcoming place; it is accessible; the patron's needs are met courteously and in a timely manner; and the environment is appropriate to the requirements of various patron groups (e.g., an active children's area; a quiet study area).

Obviously (using the trick of thinking of behaviors that would not support this type of environment), staff behaviors that are surly, insincere, judgmental, uncooperative, or disinterested are not wanted here. Behaviors that promote a welcoming, courteous, and accessible environment are expected. These desired behaviors are listed in section A of the Performance Appraisal document (Appendix D).

For example, RRPL's Code states that, "Service to the public takes precedence over the library's internal paperwork and internal communications." The philosophy or value that this Code exemplifies is that service to the library's public always comes first. The standards of performance that reflect that philosophy include: standard A3: "Acknowledges a patron's presence immediately, even if occupied"; standard A4: "Does not spend an undue amount of time or effort with one patron if another patron is waiting"; standard A11: "Puts service above any personal activities or interests while on duty"; and standard A12: "Is ready for duty at/ during scheduled times."

The employee reading these standards is able to relate these expectations for performance directly to the Code of Service. The employee knows that by meeting these specific performance standards, he or she is contributing to quality service by putting the patron's needs first. These standards clearly reflect this library's emphasis on "patron first." They also are actions or behaviors vital to daily work in a service environment.

Standards for Special and Academic Libraries

A special library's Code may say "The information center will meet the business research needs of the individual by using all available resources both within and outside the company." Suppose that one standard of performance supporting this Code is that the librarian "Regularly contacts sources successfully outside the library's collection to meet typical business informational needs." Another standard could be, "Follows through with a request for information even when no immediate response is possible." A third might be, "Establishes contacts outside the library field for retrieval of specific subject information." These standards of performance represent actions or behaviors that support this library's value of "going the extra step" to retrieve the needed information for the client.

An academic library's code may say, "The user of State College Library, whether faculty or student, is entitled to a courteous, timely response" and "The State College Library staff is committed to providing students up-to-date and relevant instruction on how to use the library." One standard derived from this code could be, "Takes responsibility for learning updated procedures for using the library" and another, "Communicates with students clearly and honestly." The employee realizes that to meet the expectations of quality service at this college library, he or she must keep current with changes in procedures and be able to inform students of these changes. For example, if the college library changes its procedures for interlibrary loan of materials from other institutions, the employee is expected to understand the revised rules and to work with students needing this service to ensure that the quality of the service does not suffer. The philosophy and the values expressed in this academic college library's code are upheld by these specific standards.

Standards Reflect Expectations

Though based on the library's role or mission, standards of performance are not a restatement of the library's role or mission. Rather, the standards are an expression of what the client or customer can expect when using the library's services and interacting with its staff. The user of the special library can expect that the librarian knows of resources outside the company which can help him. The student at the college library knows that the staff member has the most up-to-date knowledge on how to use the library and is able to communicate that knowledge clearly. Most important, the employee of the first library realizes that he or she is expected to search for contacts outside the corporate library. In the academic setting, employees know they are expected to understand, for example, how changes in the library's automated catalog system affect the use of the library and to be able to communicate those changes to the students.

External and Internal Service

If a library has a combination of staff who are strictly public service and staff who are strictly non-public service, something to be considered is whether the same standards apply to both. Rocky River Public Library made the decision that service means service to patrons *and* coworkers; the same standards apply to both. The philosophy or value behind this decision is that the entire staff works as a unit or team to support excellent service. Each staff member—whether or not he or she has direct contact with a member of the public—supports the delivery of excellent service by the whole organization. This underlying philosophy applies to the standards described in sections A and B of Appendix D, since the standards in both of these sections of the appraisal system relate directly to the overall service ethic of the library.

Overall Service and Specific Job Standards

Obviously, the job duties of staff in each segment of the library differ. Though the same performance standards of service can be applied to both public service and non-public service staff, a fair evaluation system also has to reflect the actual duties of the position. How this evaluation of specific job duties is done is illustrated in chapter 9 and in the case studies.

The complete performance evaluation document is a combination of the overall service standards and the specific job standards. The appraisal system fulfills the employee's plea to "evaluate me for what I do daily!"

Public and Non-Public Service Staff

Section A: Service to Patrons and Coworkers (Appendix D) applies, as the heading states, to both the external and internal customers of the library. The external customers are the community of users of the library—students, general public, corporate clients, faculty, children—as well as the perhaps not-so-obvious customers with whom the library staff has regular contact. For example, this section applies to how technical service staff interact with the library's book jobbers or service providers or how building service or maintenance staff interact with the individual contractors used by the library. The library's emphasis on quality service means that staff in traditionally non-public service departments have an obligation to exhibit those behaviors that promote cooperation, understanding, and communication.

The same performance standards apply to working with internal customers (coworkers). Public service staff are the customers of technical service; all departments are customers of building service. In all staff communications and interactions, the time-honored adage "treat others as you would like to be treated" definitely applies in the service environment. If staff members exhibit to one another the behaviors that produce quality service, this performance naturally reinforces the provision of quality service to the library's public.

If at all feasible, this approach of treating internal and external customers of the library the same is recommended. Both public and non-public service staff work together to support the values of the organization; they should be evaluated according to the same service standards. When using the same appraisal document for both public and nonpublic service staff, one option is to make NA or "not applicable" those few standards that truly do not apply to a particular category of staff. However, if you discover that there are more "NA" standards for one category of staff than another, or there are more "NA" standards than applicable standards, then it is time to reexamine the standards as a whole (do they truly match the code of service or mission of the library?) or to restructure the appraisal documents into separate sections for each employee category.

Applying the Standards

T he key to the success of a performance appraisal system is that it is perceived as fair by both the employee being evaluated and the employee doing the evaluating. To be accepted as fair, the performance system must be based on as an objective method of evaluation as possible. In a nonservice environment, the evaluation measurement has a tendency to be obvious—the number of products made per hour; the number of rejected pieces that have to be remade; the increase in percentage of sales per quarter. In a service environment, on the other hand, the behaviors of the employee make up his or her performance. The evaluation of the employee's performance rests on whether it matches the expected level of service the library strives to provide.

Removing Chances for Subjectivity

How is it possible to make the evaluation of behaviors as objective as possible? First, it is essential to remove as many opportunities for subjectivity as can be identified.

If an evaluation is required once a year, the worse possible scenario is to ask a supervisor to sit down at the end of the appraisal period (with no prior reviews with the employee) with a checklist of traits and evaluate the employee by marking off "poor," "fair," "good," or "excellent" or by circling numbers on a scale. The employee then reads the evaluation and is either lectured on his or her need to improve or told he is "doing a good job."

In this scenario, because of human nature, the supervisor most probably will be marking off and circling based on the employee's most recent behavior. Heaven help the employee who just had an angry exchange with an irate patron! That encounter is what will stick in the supervisor's mind, regardless of prior behavior. Or, the supervisor will base his or her evaluation on the overall impression of the employee and his reputation in the organization. Oh, I remember Sue wrote that wonderful report the director loved . . . or Mary never causes any problems and is a steady, loyal worker. The supervisor is evaluating not actual performance, but rather his or her *impression* of the employee, which might or might not be accurate. For example, Sue did write that wonderful report—but maybe it was the only wonderful thing she did all year. Mary is a steady, self-effacing worker, but does the supervisor remember her suggestions for simplifying the ordering process?

Quirks in Rating Scales and Checklists

There also is a tendency for a supervisor to rate the employees in the middle of any scale. One, it is easier for a supervisor to avoid having to deal with someone disappointed by a poor rating. Two, it can be less stressful for the supervisor not to single someone out for excellent performance. Using a checklist or a circle-the-numbers rating system also does not eliminate the personal tendencies in rating among supervisors. Sometime in your career you probably have had a supervisor who has stated, "I never give 10s because no one is perfect," or a supervisor who could not possibly give anyone a poor rating since, "there is some good in everyone."

The once-a-year checklist approach is comparably fast and easy, but does it accomplish the goal of providing quality service in the library? Such a method would certainly not be perceived as fair by the library staff, since each supervisor is using his or her own views rather than specific criteria for making the final judgment. No common standard is being applied to ensure that the expected quality of performance is being reinforced. Actual performance throughout the year is not being reviewed, so accountability to the library's public cannot be claimed. Most important, the opportunity for the employee to understand how he or she is meeting (or not meeting) the expectations for performance is lost. Though not impossible, it is difficult for an employee to improve his or her performance if the organization does not devote the time, attention, and resources to helping him do so.

Guidelines Promote Fairness

In using the complete performance appraisal system described in this manual, both the employee and the supervisor know what is expected for the everyday delivery of quality service, and the standards of performance relate directly to the employee's daily activities.

To provide a structure to support fairness, each standard has its own set of guidelines (see chapter 5), which are specific criteria upon which the employee can be objectively evaluated. When evaluating an employee, the supervisor uses the guidelines for each standard to prevent subjective tendencies. The guidelines for the standards are statements that clearly define the expected behaviors for "meets standard," "exceeds standard," and "needs improvement." The supervisor cannot indiscriminately rate an employee high—or low—across the board or base the appraisal on impressions. The statements in the guidelines provide a clear picture of what the library expects. Using these guidelines, both employee and supervisor are considering the level of the employee's performance in the same manner.

Standards of Performance Guidelines

The Standards of Performance Guidelines document (Appendix B) clarifies the standards of performance to ensure that each supervisor is evaluating performance at the same level.

Three Levels of Performance

For each standard there are three possible levels of performance: "meets standard," "exceeds standard," or "needs improvement." For the evaluation process to be judged as fair by staff, each supervisor's definition of the level of the employee's behavior must be aligned with other supervisors' definitions. The Standards of Performance Guidelines document describes the level of behavior or activity that determines whether an employee meets, does not meet, or exceeds a standard. The examples given in the Guidelines typify actual behaviors of employees in a library service environment, with varying levels illustrated.

Example: Standard A1

For example, supporting the emphasis on friendly and courteous service as outlined in the Code, the first standard of performance in section A, "Service to Patrons and Coworkers," is "Makes eye contact, greets others sincerely, and speaks in a friendly manner."

From this standard (and others in section A), it is evident that Rocky River Public Library expects its staff to create a friendly environment in which a patron's presence is welcomed and acknowledged. It is not expected that a staff member consistently seek out patrons to ask them what they need. The guidelines for this standard (see Appendix B) give specific examples of behaviors for the levels of "meets standard," "exceeds standard," and "needs improvement" to assist the supervisor in evaluating the employee.

Standard A1

Makes eye contact, greets others sincerely, and speaks in a friendly manner.

Meets Standard	You greet all patrons and coworkers politely.
	You immediately look up when patrons or coworkers approach and greet them warmly.
	You recognize frequent patrons.
	You speak in a friendly manner to all staff.
Exceeds Standard	You maintain a consistently friendly manner with difficult patrons or staff.
	You are able to acknowledge and carry on a friendly conversation with most of the patrons with whom you have contact.
Needs Improvement	You are frequently unpleasant (e.g., you rarely smile; you have an abrupt manner; you make someone feel he or she is annoying you).
	You do not look up when someone approaches.
	You only occasionally smile and make eye contact.
	You are pleasant only to people you like or know.

The supervisor uses his or her own wording in the documentation of behavior—always following the examples in the Standards of Performance Guidelines document to determine the level of the behavior. The supervisor is not required to use the examples given in the Guidelines—only the level of behavior that the examples represent. The library administration, supervisors, and staff have, through writing the Guidelines, determined what level of behavior meets each standard. That level of understanding for "meets standard" then determines the deviation from that standard for "needs improvement" and "exceeds standard."

These Guidelines are a key part of ensuring that the performance appraisal system is perceived by all involved as fair. The Guidelines are those of the library as a whole, rather than one individual's definition of the standards of performance.

Example: Standard A14

Let's look at standard A14 and its guidelines to examine more closely the differing levels of behavior for "meets standard," "exceeds standard," and "needs improvement."

From the actions or behaviors listed for each category, both employee and supervisor can understand the level of performance that is expected. To meet this standard, the employee keeps informed and uses work-provided means to learn updated procedures. An employee not meeting

---

Standard A14

Takes responsibility for learning updated internal procedures.

Meets Standard	You attend meetings regularly.
	If you are not sure about a procedure, you make it a point to get the correct information.
	You read minutes of meetings, memos, and e-mail.
	You are current with organizational safety procedures and are able to immediately locate the departmental safety manual.
Exceeds Standard	You immediately alert the appropriate person of safety concerns and follow through with solutions or implementations of procedures.
	You take the initiative to inform coworkers of changes in procedures when you observe that updated procedures are not being followed.
	Other staff consistently look to you for answers on updated procedures.
	You are actively involved in development of or training in safety and security matters.
Needs Improvement	You are not informed about the activities in your department.
	You do not read memos or e-mail regularly.
	You are unaware of organizational safety procedures and may not remember where to locate the departmental safety manual.

---

this standard does not keep informed and does not make a regular effort to learn updated procedures (e.g., does not attend meetings, does not read memos or e-mail messages regularly). To exceed this standard, an employee goes beyond being informed and knowledgeable about updated procedures and actively uses his or her knowledge to enhance or improve service. For example, the employee actually participates in the development of new procedures through suggesting changes or is a resource person to whom staff naturally turn for help with new procedures.

A Supervisor's Comments

Again, a supervisor writing comments for the employee's evaluation does *not* have to use the examples given in the Standards of Performance Guidelines. The supervisor *does* use examples of the employee's behavior that match the *levels* of behavior illustrated in the Guidelines. A supervisor of a reference librarian may comment that the employee exceeds standard A14 because she shared with her colleagues printed aids that she developed on her own. The explanation of the comment would include mention of the notebook of departmental procedures the librarian compiled and the instances in which other staff found it useful.

A supervisor who is evaluating an employee might comment that the employee is not meeting this standard because the employee has shown a pattern of behavior that demonstrates he is not informed about new procedures directly related to his work. For example, for a circulation department employee, the supervisor states that the employee consistently does not know about updated circulation procedures that have been explained at department meetings, in memos, or on e-mail. On numerous occasions the employee has not been able to update a patron's registration record under the new system. The employee consistently does not ask for assistance when he does not know something and reverts to doing it the outdated way. Or, conversely, a supervisor might comment that the circulation department employee exceeds this standard since, on several occasions over a period of time, the supervisor has noted that other staff consistently turn to that employee for help when they are confused or hesitant about new procedures. The employee not only knows the new procedures, but is able consistently to assist other staff in implementing them to improve service.

Patterns of Behavior

The writers of the Rocky River Public Library Guidelines deliberately avoided the words "never" and "always." It is unrealistic to think that an employee could always do something or never make a mistake or act inappropriately. It is just not humanly possible in the real world. Because this performance appraisal system is based on evaluating daily work in a service environment, "often," "frequently," and "consistently" convey the tone of the expected level of behavior. The supervisor is looking for a pattern of behavior rather than focusing on isolated incidents.

Coaching

Since this complete performance appraisal system reflects and reinforces the library's values and delivery of quality service, a main purpose of the evaluation process is to coach any employees not providing the expected quality of service. The goal is for the employee to reach a "meets standard" or "exceeds standard" for each performance standard in the document. A "meets standards" evaluation means the employee is providing the high level of quality service the library expects. An "exceeds standards" evaluation indicates that the employee substantially surpasses the expected level of service with little or no prompting. As a coaching tool, the appraisal document is the framework within which the supervisor and the employee work together to improve the employee's performance to a "meets" or "exceeds" level.

The Goal Is to Meet or Exceed Standards

It is the responsibility of both the employee and the supervisor to work together toward the same goal of meeting or exceeding standards to provide the best service possible to coworkers or to the library's customers. If a pattern of "exceeds standard" develops, the supervisor notes specific instances to illustrate that excellence. The documenting of excellent performance behaviors also is an "on-the-job" opportunity for the supervisor to give direct and immediate praise or recognition to that employee. If an employee is "needs improvement" for one or more standards, then the supervisor and the employee agree on a plan that will permit the employee to reach a "meets standard" before the end of the appraisal period.

Seeing a Pattern

Evaluation for any standard of performance is not based on single, unrelated actions, but rather on a continuing series of instances that have been observed and documented by the supervisor. The supervisor must see a *pattern*—whether it is a pattern of behavior that exceeds the standard or a pattern that does not meet the standard. One extraordinary act of excellent service delivery does not mean an "exceeds standard" for the employee; conversely, one mistake or inappropriate encounter does not doom the employee to a "needs improvement" for that standard. Two consistent actions or behaviors (in a relatively short period of time) relating to the performance for a standard alerts the supervisor to the employee's departure from a "meets standard." The supervisor works with the employee to improve performance by pointing out alternative actions or behaviors the employee should be using. If the performance does not alter to the supervisor's satisfaction, the supervisor begins documenting instances to determine whether the pattern persists.

No End-of-Year Surprises!

Again, it is important to emphasize that any employee whom a supervisor determines is not meeting a standard should not be surprised by that evaluation at the end of the appraisal period. Since one of the main points of this performance appraisal system is to maintain a level of service consistent with the library's Code of Service and the standards derived from its values, the goal of the supervisor is to help each employee meet or exceed standards. An employee not meeting one or more standards is first informed of the need to improve by his or her supervisor, and then coached through an action plan to succeed. Instead of an "end-of-year" surprise, the employee knows throughout the year what is expected and how he or she is meeting those expectations.

Action Plan

Once a supervisor perceives that an employee is having difficulty meeting a standard of performance, the supervisor is obligated to discuss with the employee what action is needed to meet that standard. Meetings for an action plan are on an "as needed" basis and are in addition to the scheduled evaluation reviews. When an employee's behaviors need improvement, the supervisor and the employee agree upon an appropriate action plan. The supervisor and the employee decide on the time and resources needed to meet the standard. That action plan is written on the document to ensure that both supervisor and employee agree to the steps needed for change in the behavior.

The Plan Emphasizes Positive Behaviors

An action plan emphasizes positive behavior and is designed to help the employee deliver quality service. If done correctly, *with cooperation from both the supervisor and the employee*, the result will be a "meets standard," not a "needs improvement." The action plan can be as simple as, "you will check in with your supervisor upon arrival" for the employee who is not ready for duty at scheduled times. The checking-in process alerts the supervisor to any continuing pattern of tardiness or unreadiness. Or the action plan could be more extensive, requiring the employee to attend a refresher course on an aspect of the job for which she is not meeting standards or to spend time each day reviewing a certain function with which she is having difficulty. The action plan could include a step which mandates that the employee illustrate her competence in a particular function or activity to the supervisor.

Action Plan Steps

If the employee and the supervisor cannot come to a mutually agreeable plan of action, then the next level of management assists. The director or executive officer is the final arbiter. The employee has the responsibility to follow the action plan and to consult with the supervisor if difficulties in fulfilling the intent of the plan arise. There can be either a specific action plan for one standard (noted next to that standard on the performance document) or an overall action plan encompassing many standards (noted on the "comments" page of the document).

7

Reviews of
Performance

O ngoing communication and reinforcement of positive behaviors are essential tools for effective coaching. How many times the supervisor and the employee meet to review the progress of the employee's performance is determined by the library's situation. If the organization of the library makes it convenient for the supervisor and the employee to communicate privately on a regular basis, then it is less important to have in place a predetermined number of formal review meetings.

What is most critical is the opportunity for the employee and the supervisor to exchange information in a private setting, with no interruptions. This performance appraisal system is effective since it provides a framework of objectivity and fairness within which relevant discussion on behaviors can occur. However, if a library does not devote the time to implementing the system, the benefits of the performance appraisal system decrease.

Effective Feedback

Private time set aside for the employee and the supervisor to exchange information results in effective feedback for both the supervisor and the employee. Using the Standards of Performance Guidelines (see chapter 5), the supervisor is able to give concrete examples of behavior for reinforcement or improvement of performance. The supervisor can be very specific without becoming personal, since the examples are based on work-related behaviors and actions and the behaviors are evaluated according to library-wide standards. The review meeting is also an opportunity for the employee to recall and communicate to the supervisor actions that resulted in quality service. For both employee and supervisor, the review is an optimal occasion for listening and learning about performance concerns. What support the employee needs from the library and what changes in behavior the supervisor is expecting from the employee are key issues to discuss.

Review Meetings

Regardless of what works best for a particular library—a series of scheduled progress meetings or scheduled reviews with additional meetings added "as needed"—it is very important to have at a minimum a formal mid-year review, in addition to the final appraisal. Do not depend only on a once-a-year, final evaluation review. A mid-year review provides the opportunity for employee and supervisor to sit down in a private setting to exchange notes about the employee's performance.

Obviously, if a supervisor has determined that an employee "needs improvement" in one or more standards, the supervisor and the employee will be meeting more frequently, first to set a plan of action and then to review the employee's progress toward improvement.

What Is Discussed

If an employee is at "meets standards" or "exceeds standards," the mid-year review (or any other regularly scheduled meeting) is an opportunity for the employee and supervisor to reexamine goals related to the employee's job. It is also an occasion for the supervisor to commend the employee on his or her performance (for reinforcement of behaviors) and for the employee to share problems and concerns.

In addition, the performance review meeting is an opportunity for the supervisor and the employee to discuss the kinds of changes that will be occurring in the department over the next year and in what ways those changes will affect how the employee does his or her job. Perhaps the special library will be taking on a priority project requiring more flexible scheduling for speedy completion. Or the academic library has the responsibility to develop a collection for a new course added to the undergraduate curriculum. The public library may be undergoing a major change—cutbacks in services; an extensive remodeling; or an automation project. These changes demand adjustments in the work flow and affect the expectations for each employee's performance. The formal review meetings strengthen the channel of communication between supervisor and employee to prevent any surprises or "You should have known want I wanted" criticisms.

Any performance reviews prior to the final one should be used to discuss the standards of performance to verify that the employee knows what is expected of him or her. The initial meeting (or the end-of-year review meeting) should be used to set any goals for the employee. These goals are part of the supervisor's comments at the end of the performance document. Again, it is a written confirmation of the supervisor's expectations for performance within a person's specific job duties.

Determining the Number of Review Meetings

After using this appraisal system for several years, RRPL has found that a formal mid-year and final review are sufficient for effective coaching. It is recommended that supervisors add a review at the beginning of the appraisal year for any new employees who have not yet gone through the process. This initial meeting is needed to verify that the new employee completely understands the standards by which he or she will be evaluated. The Supervisory Procedures for Conducting a Performance Evaluation (Appendix C) state that, "additional performance meetings are held during the year with individual employees, as needed." If an employee is having difficulty meeting a standard, additional meetings throughout the year may be used for reinforcement or adjustment of the action plan.

First Meeting Useful for Solid Start

A library just starting to use this performance appraisal system should seriously consider keeping a formal meeting at the beginning of the appraisal period until its staff is comfortable with the coaching focus of this evaluation process. During this first meeting, the supervisor and the employee review the performance document together, using the Standards of Performance Guidelines (Appendix B) as the starting point for discussion of expected levels of performance. Any questions about what is expected of the employee—and the supervisor—are answered. For example, an employee might state that she or he thinks there is a need for more resources (time or training) to meet a particular standard. If the supervisor disagrees, there is an opportunity for resolution of differences through consultation with the next level of management. Any misunderstanding about what is expected jeopardizes a fair evaluation of the employee and makes the job of the supervisor more difficult. Use the first formal review meeting to clarify the expectations; then the mid-year review can focus on the employee's specific performance in meeting the standards.

Coaching Directly Related to Job

All this talk about coaching, meeting, and action plans makes the performance appraisal process sound much more complicated than it truly is. Since this performance appraisal system is based on evaluating "what we do daily" in a service environment, the coaching is directly related to what an employee should be doing on the job. If the employee is exhibiting behaviors not consistent with the library's values, it will be readily apparent. The supervisor and the employee then use the Standards of Performance document as the objective framework within which to discuss the discrepancy in behavior and how to remedy it. The Standards document helps remove the possibility that the employee sees the request to improve as a personal attack by the supervisor. The employee realizes that all employees are evaluated using the same standards. Supervisors appreciate this performance appraisal system because they are implementing library-wide, consistent, and objective standards of performance.

Since this performance appraisal system is based on coaching throughout the appraisal period, the fear or perceived difficulty of either doing or receiving a final evaluation is lessened. The supervisor, throughout the appraisal period, has either been reinforcing positive behaviors or setting up action plans for unsatisfactory behaviors, based on the standards of performance. There are no surprises at the final evaluation review, making it less stressful for both employee and supervisor. Employees know that each supervisor is using the same set of standards and that they are being evaluated fairly.

Supervisory Procedures

To further guarantee that all supervisors are following a standard set by the library, a procedural outline is helpful (see Supervisory Procedures for Conducting a Performance Evaluation, Appendix C). The Supervisory Procedures sheet indicates the time frame for performance reviews. For flexibility (especially for public service departments when public demands on staff time is sometimes unpredictable), setting a range of weeks or months as the deadline for the reviews (e.g., by March 31 or by July 31) relieves the stress of having to accomplish a number of reviews within a week's time.

The Supervisory Procedures for Conducting a Performance Evaluation sheet also reinforces what is to be accomplished at the review: the discussion of both strengths (with examples) and behaviors that need improvement (with examples), as applicable; the agreement on an action plan, if needed; the verification of what action, if any, is expected of the employee.

Also noted in the Supervisory Procedures is the requirement that an employee's performance of his or her specific job duties must be "meets standards" for the employee to receive an overall performance rating of "meets standards" or "exceeds standards."

The Supervisory Procedures sheet, through outlining the steps involved in conducting a performance evaluation and outlining in black and white the timetable for the review, helps to ensure that all supervisors are conducting the mechanics of the performance reviews in the same manner.

New Employees

As noted earlier, in libraries that require only one mid-year meeting before the final evaluation, it is recommended there be a third, beginning of the appraisal year, meeting for a new employee. This third meeting is used to review the standards, answer questions about expectations, set any specific job goals, and explain the appraisal process. This meeting is time well spent since it provides an opportunity to allay any misapprehensions about how and when the employee is to be evaluated.

Appraisal Period

It is important to decide whether the appraisal period begins on the anniversary date of the employee (i.e., the date the employee joined the organization) or begins for all employees on the same date in the calendar year. The number of staff, the number of supervisors, the demands from the library's public, the patterns of work flow, and whether the employee's performance appraisal is tied to his or her annual compensation are factors in deciding when the appraisal period begins.

If the appraisal period for all employees begins on the same date (e.g., January 1), then consideration must be made for those new employees who start in the middle of or toward the end of the calendar year. Questions to ask are: Is a new employee included in the annual appraisal if he or she was not employed at the start of the appraisal period; if so, what is the cutoff point for participation? An employee must be given a reasonable period of time in which to meet or exceed the performance standards. It is hardly fair either to the new employee or to the other staff to evaluate the new employee on a relatively short period of employment. If a new employee is not evaluated during the current appraisal period, is there any provision to use the performance standards to monitor performance during a probationary evaluation period or, if the evaluation is tied to compensation, to recognize the employee's performance in another way?

Example of an Appraisal Time Period

At RRPL, since the evaluation is tied directly to compensation, the minimum period of time for an effective evaluation is six months. The appraisal period starts January 1. An employee who begins employment at RRPL January 1 through June 30 is included in the current year's performance evaluation process. An employee who begins employment at RRPL July 1 through December 31 is included in the current year's performance evaluation process only if the supervisor determines the need to coach performance to reach an acceptable level. An employee who begins employment at RRPL July 1 through December 31 whose performance is at an acceptable level as determined by his or her supervisor will not receive a merit level increase but is eligible for a one-time performance bonus (prorated for actual employment time). This option is one way to recognize the efforts of new employees while still being fair to the other staff. It certainly is not the only option, and an individual library's policy should be tailored to the specific library's situation.

Documenting Behavior

A s noted, this complete performance appraisal system is based on what a library employee does on a daily basis. Consequently, the evaluation process occurs throughout the appraisal period, rather than as a last-minute scramble to come up with a final assessment. The best (and easiest for the supervisor) way to accomplish the goal of evaluating an employee on behaviors throughout the year, rather than on the last few weeks of the appraisal period, is for the supervisor to document any pattern of deviation from "meets standard."

Noting Patterns of Behavior

Throughout the year, the supervisor notes specific, observed actions or behaviors of the employee. Each supervisor may have a different method of tracking patterns of behavior. One of the most effective methods seems to be a calendar or diary on which a supervisor can note reminders of employees' actions. Another is a folder into which the supervisor slips notes or memos.

These reminders or notes are used as the "examples of behavior" in the performance document to reflect the true (rather than perceived) actions of the employee. Again, it is important to emphasize that the supervisor is not noting isolated incidents, but rather a series of continuing actions which document that the employee is either exceeding a standard or needs improvement.

What to Document

The supervisor has the option of documenting or not documenting "meets standard" behaviors. It is left up to the supervisor to determine if she or he has the time to do so. The supervisor *must* document, with examples of specific, observed actions, any pattern of continuing behavior that falls into the category of "needs improvement" or "exceeds standard." Since a supervisor cannot be at all places at all times, it is permissible for the departmental supervisor to use examples of behaviors noted by other supervisors. In a library setting, this option can occur during weekend or evening hours when a departmental supervisor may not be scheduled, but there is a designated or building supervisor on duty. Whenever possible, the departmental supervisor, when alerted by another supervisor that an employee is deviating from "meets standard" on a consistent basis, should make it a point either to observe similar situations during which the suspected behavior may occur, or to sit down with the employee to discuss the implications of the comments the supervisor has received.

Ideally, it would be wonderful if an employee would alert the supervisor to any actions that indicate the employee is exceeding a standard. Experience has shown that this self-awareness is not the norm for most employees. However, comments from other employees to the supervisor, from supervisor to supervisor, or general e-mail messages or library-wide communications do alert the supervisor to "exceeds standard" behavior, which the supervisor can then observe and document for examples of behavior in the final evaluation.

Examples of Behavior

The examples of behavior are a vital part of this complete performance appraisal system. They illustrate, in real-life terms, why the employee is either not meeting, or exceeding, the standards. The Standards of Performance Guidelines document (Appendix B) provides the *interpretation* the supervisor uses to note whether the employee's actions are at the level of meeting, exceeding, or not meeting the standards. For the individual employee, the supervisor uses whatever examples of behavior best illustrate a continuing pattern of "exceeds" or "needs improvement"— and is not tied to the examples given in the Guidelines since they are illustrative only. For standard A5, a supervisor may note an employee's "exceeds standard" behaviors by using an example such as the following, which is not included in the Guidelines but which fits the level of activity necessary for an "exceeds standard": "You show creativity and initiative in finding interesting and informative programming sources loved by the children (e.g., the Native American dancers; the live bat program from the Natural History Museum; and the talk from a real lighthouse keeper").

When discussing examples of "on-the-job" behaviors that match the levels depicted in the Guidelines, both employee and supervisor are "speaking the same language." The discussion is objective, rather than accusatory or based on impressions. And, if necessary, an action plan can provide the means for an employee to meet a standard before the final evaluation.

Specific Job
Standards

An important part of this complete performance appraisal system is the evaluation of specific job duties. This section of the appraisal is so vital that it is weighted as half (50 percent) of the total evaluation. If an employee is also a supervisor, the standards for supervision (Appendix D, section D) and the Specific Job Standards (Appendix D, section C) are combined to equal half (50 percent) of the final evaluation.

Importance of Job Duties
in the Evaluation

In order for an employee to receive an overall performance appraisal of "meets standards" or "exceeds standards," the employee must have at least a minimum "meets standards" rating for his or her position responsibilities. An employee who has several "needs improvement" ratings for specific job duties on the final evaluation should, as part of the coaching process, already have action plans in place which he or she has been trying to meet. If the final evaluation results in an overall "needs improvement" in the job duties section, then serious consideration must be given to separating the employee from the organization. The basic premise is that an employee must be able to perform the job duties at a "meets standards" level, no matter how wonderfully he or she may be meeting the other standards (Appendix D, sections A and B).

Specific Standards for Job Duties

Some libraries do have specific standards for each job category. These specific job standards could be listed in section C of the performance document. RRPL, on the other hand, bases the standards for section C, Specific Job Standards, on the employee's position description. The supervisor distills the job description into four or five major duties or responsibilities that encompass the specific duties listed in the job description. These major duties and responsibilities must be the same for all employees in the same job category. Using the system of comments and examples of behavior, the supervisor notes any deviation from "meets standard." If an employee has a "needs improvement" in one or more of those duties, the supervisor and employee work together to initiate an action plan for improving performance. "Needs improvement" in all of the duties and responsibilities of the position is a sign of a very serious problem that should be addressed aggressively by the supervisor according to the individual library's procedures for dealing with inadequate job performance (e.g., probationary period; personnel policy procedures that deal with reasons for termination).

Examples of Behavior for Job Duties

The comments and examples of behavior for the specific job duties reflect either the extra effort an employee puts into the actual job duties or the lack of effort that does not produce the minimum expected. Since the examples of behavior come from the daily activities of the department, the next level of management (or director) can readily evaluate supervisors' levels of expectation. Expectations that are too low—or too high—could certainly require a discussion of the library's goals with any of the supervisors. Of course, the supervisors also are part of the same evaluation process, with a separate section devoted exclusively to supervisory standards (see chapter 10). One of the supervisory standards is standard D8: "Documents performance, then evaluates staff objectively and constructively, and in a timely manner."

Writing Standards for Specific Jobs

As mentioned above, it is possible to write standards for specific job duties which could become section C of the performance appraisal document (Appendix D). However, a component of writing those specific job standards is the weighting of each job duty according to the amount of time the employee spends on each one. For example, a custodian may have janitorial and maintenance tasks inside the building, duties outside the building (including grass cutting, parking lot cleaning, and snow removal), the responsibility of doing repairs upon demand, and also be expected to assist with the physical inventory. If there are standards for each of these duties (e.g., the grass is to be cut once a week during the growing season; the weeds are to be pulled twice a week; the physical inventory is to be at least 95 percent accurate), they must be weighted according to the relevance of the task in a daily schedule, how much time could be assigned realistically to each task for the number of hours the employee works, and the significance or importance of each task for library operations.

In place of the weighting of each job duty, the system described in this manual uses the job description for the basis of section C of the appraisal document. With the comments and examples of behavior, it provides a workable method that is fair to all the employees in the same job category. Compare the job descriptions included in the case studies with the major job duties listed in the employee's performance appraisal document for an understanding of how the specific job duties are derived.

Whether a library uses specific standards for the job duties (e.g., the number of items processed in an hour; the percentage of informational questions answered accurately; the number of bibliographic instruction classes held) or uses the job description itself, the comments and examples of behavior taken from the observations of daily work make the evaluation meaningful for both employee and supervisor.

Goal Setting

Often, and especially for jobs with higher levels of responsibility, the supervisor will want to set goals for the employee for the upcoming year. In this performance appraisal system, the goals are set during the first review meeting of the appraisal year. If there are only mid-year and final review meetings, then the goals are set at the final meeting of the current year for the upcoming appraisal period.

The goals are set during a review meeting so that the supervisor and employee have the opportunity to discuss the intent of the goals, what is expected of the employee in fulfilling the goals, and what resources (time, money, support) are required for providing the necessary environment for success. The goals are written in the supervisor's comments or as an addendum attached to the document. As the year progresses, the supervisor notes comments and examples of behavior relating to the goals in the performance document, either under the appropriate standard in sections A and B, or in section C: Specific Job Standards (Appendix D).

10

Supervisory Standards

O ften (especially in small to medium-sized libraries), a supervisor is a "working" supervisor. The supervisor not only manages a department or function, but also is responsible for specific job duties. For example, the head of technical services hires, evaluates, and supervises staff; schedules staff and work flow; runs reports and does administrative paperwork (including ordering supplies); and serves on the library's management team. Yet the head of technical services also has the specific job duties of classifying and cataloging the library's collections. The head of informational or reference services has "on-the-floor" public service duties as well as managerial or supervisory responsibilities. The head of building services supervises employees, but also is required to perform the job duties of cutting grass, repairing equipment, plowing the parking lot in winter, or handling deliveries, just as his or her employees do.

Expectations for Supervisors

For evaluation purposes, the expectations for supervisory responsibilities are in section D: Supervisory Standards (Appendix D). The corresponding guidelines for these standards are in the Standards of Performance Guidelines document (Appendix B). The job duties (taken from the job description of the supervisor) are in section C: Specific Job Standards. For the overall evaluation of a supervisor, sections C and D are combined to weigh as half (50 percent) of the final evaluation. For nonsupervisory staff, section C: Specific Job Standards, is half of the final evaluation.

Separate Supervisory Standards

For the "working" or "on-floor" supervisor, both supervisory and specific job duties comprise his or her job. Having a separate section for just supervisory standards, however, permits a library-wide consistency in what is expected of all supervisors. Whether the supervisor is public service (circulation services) or non-public (technical services), the expectations for supervision are the same. For example, all supervisors are expected to make appropriate decisions (standard D2); resolve problems fairly (standard D3); and work effectively with staff to improve performance (standard D7), regardless of their specific job duties.

Relate Standards to Goals and Projects

For each of the supervisory standards, the Standards of Performance Guidelines document (Appendix B) gives examples of behavior to indicate what level of activity or behavior is "meets standard," "exceeds standard," or "needs improvement." Because of the relatively higher scale of responsibilities of supervisors, the comments and examples of behavior in the performance document often relate to actions and behaviors within a more complex context of goals or projects. Standard D9 states that a supervisor "actively coordinates with other departments." Whether that supervisor "meets," "exceeds," or "needs improvement" for this standard often is determined by how effectively a goal is reached or a project accomplished.

Perhaps there is a library-wide goal of adding a new format to the library's collections (e.g., a circulating computer software and CD-ROM collection) to meet a growing demand from the library's public. Such a collection fits within the library's mission and within the mandates of its Code to provide accessible, current, and relevant materials for loan. How the head of technical services handles the staffing, work flow, and cooperative issues surrounding the implementation of this goal will be reflected in the comments and examples not only for standard D9, but probably also standards D1, D3, D4, and D6.

Example of Supervisory "Exceeds Standard"

An ES or "exceeds standard" comment for a head of technical services charged with adding a new format could state, "You have been very willing to cooperate with other departments on various projects, including the integration of the new formats of computer software and CD-ROM packages into our circulating AV collection." Examples of ES behavior might include such observations as, "You worked closely with both circulation services and audiovisual services on the most effective packaging for computer software to reduce the handling of these items during the check-out and check-in functions" (standard D9). "You verified with audiovisual services what labeling was needed on the packages to explain copyright laws and virus protection; you offered suggestions and worked with audiovisual services to develop readable, understandable labeling" (standard D9). "You integrated the classifying, cataloging, and processing of these new formats (CD-ROM and computer software) into your department's work flow without creating an unreasonable backlog or delaying the processing of other formats" (standard D6).

Example of Supervisory "Needs Improvement"

An NI or "needs improvement" comment for the same situation could be, "You refused to cooperate with either circulation services or audiovisual services on the most effective way of processing the new formats of CD-ROM and computer software circulating items, resulting in a major delay of implementing this new service." Examples of NI behavior could include observations of behaviors such as, "You delayed meeting with key staff in both circulation services and audiovisual services to discuss packaging and labeling of the new format of CD-ROM and computer software packages; instead of offering suggestions for ways to move ahead with the project, you refused to adjust your staff's work flow to accommodate the processing of this format" (standard D9).

Supervisory Standards and Job Duties Interrelated

Because of the complexity and scope of the projects and goals at the supervisory level, often comments and examples of behavior relating to the project will appear under both the supervisory standards and the specific job duties. In section C: Specific Job Standards for head of technical services, a major job duty is "Manages the daily operation of the technical services department." Using the example given above, an NI comment would be, "You have not cataloged or processed the formats of CD-ROM and computer software packages in a timely or efficient manner and have delayed the implementation of this service for our public." Examples of NI behavior include, "You have created a backlog of items waiting to be cataloged and processed because of your unwillingness to work with other departments." An ES comment is, "You have streamlined and consolidated duties to meet the changing formats being added to the collections." An ES example of behavior is, "Your management of the department has resulted in no backlog of either the new or already existing formats." An MS or "meets standard" comment is, "You have integrated the new formats of CD-ROM and computer software packages with minimal disruption of service."

For the specific job duty of "Manages the daily operation of the technical services department," one of the differences between "meets standard," "exceeds standard," and "needs improvement" is that the head of technical services has either integrated a new format with minimal disruption, integrated the new format with no disruption through an efficient reorganization of the work flow, or totally delayed the implementation of this new service through stonewalling and inaction.

The Overall Evaluation

O ne of the major benefits of this complete performance appraisal system is that it limits the opportunity for the supervisor to fit the evaluation to a preconceived notion of an employee's performance. Each supervisor must follow the levels of activity or behavior that are indicated in the Standards of Performance Guidelines (Appendix B). The examples of behavior from the employee's on-the-job performance must reflect the levels of behavior, whether they are "meets standard," "exceeds standard," or "needs improvement" as indicated by the Guidelines. In fact, without the risk of preconception, sometimes a supervisor is genuinely surprised, at the tabulation stage, to find that an employee has contributed so much extra effort over the year!

A second major benefit is that the performance document indicates, in an objective manner, areas needing improvement. The supervisor notes specific examples to illustrate why the employee is not meeting a standard. The employee and the supervisor devise a plan for the employee to meet the standard, and the supervisor and library management provide the resources to assist the employee. The intent is to improve the quality of service being delivered by the employee. As indicated in the introduction to this manual, evaluating quality in a service environment relates directly to what the employee does on a daily basis. Ensuring that the individual employee understands what is expected for quality service, and providing the opportunity for the employee to succeed in meeting that expected level of service, results in overall quality service for the library's users.

How Is the Annual Review Used?

Ultimately, the performance appraisal process results in the employee's annual performance review and rating. It is up to the individual library to decide how that annual evaluation document is used. Is it a coaching tool only? Is it tied directly to the employee's compensation? Is it used as a means for distributing bonus or nonsalary increases? Is it one indicator of promotion possibilities?

At RRPL, the annual evaluation is tied directly to the employee's compensation. As of this writing, salary increases are merit only, based on the individual's job performance. There is no across-the-board or automatic cost-of-living increase. This particular library has strongly connected service and accountability to its public with compensation of its employees.

Tabulating the Overall Rating

To be fair—and as objective as possible—to each employee, the overall rating for the employee's annual performance evaluation is scored according to a standard form. Originally, it was thought that a supervisor could just tell (from the number of "meets standard," "exceeds standard," or "needs improvement" ratings given to an employee) whether an employee fell into one of those categories overall. However, once again, the supervisors believed that method was not objective enough. What if one supervisor felt that "needs improvement" in three service standards meant an overall "needs improvement" and another supervisor thought five was the determining number?

Instead, the supervisors and administration devised rating points for each category to ensure that all supervisors apply the same criteria to all employees. At RRPL, the performance rating system is a "three-point" system. For each standard an "exceeds standard" (ES) equals 3 points; a "meets standard" (MS) equals 2 points; and a "needs improvement" (NI) equals 1 point.

After a supervisor has written the comments and examples of behavior according to the Standards of Performance Guidelines, he or she goes back to the document and, using the tabulation sheet (Appendix E), counts all the MS, ES, and NI points. The supervisor transfers that information directly to the tabulation sheet. The tabulation sheet may look complicated, but it is not! Instead, it takes the supervisor step-by-step through the tabulation process. The supervisor merely "plugs in" the numbers to determine the overall rating.

Number of Standards That Apply

The tabulation takes into account the number of standards that apply to the employee (since in section A: Service to Patrons and Coworkers it is possible that one or more standards may not apply to nonpublic service employees) before tallying the total for that section. It also divides the total performance points into two equal sections: Service and Personal Development are combined into one section; and Specific Job Standards (or, if the employee is a supervisor, Specific Job Standards and Supervisory Standards) is the other half. For actual examples, see the tabulation sheets for each of the employee case studies included in this manual.

This precise way of tabulating the employee's annual performance rating protects the evaluation's objectivity for each employee and assures that all supervisors are following one library-wide procedure.

Introduction

This complete performance appraisal system is based on evaluating quality of performance in a service environment. Its premise is that if a library wants to have its performance appraisal system reinforced and support the delivery of quality service, then the library must state and communicate its expectations (the standards of performance) to its employees and then apply those standards fairly and objectively to all staff (Standards of Performance Guidelines).

Structure of the Case Studies

The case studies that follow illustrate the implementation of the complete performance appraisal system described in this manual. Each case study has an introduction describing the particular focus (e.g., whether the evaluation illustrates coaching a new employee or is of a long-term staff member), a profile of the employee illustrating typical actions or behaviors, the employee's position description, the performance evaluation itself with comments and examples of behavior, and the tabulation sheet that gives the overall performance rating for that employee. All of the documents presented in these case studies are included as appendixes at the end of this book.

Case Studies Reflect Real-Life Situations

These case studies are included to give a library contemplating using this performance appraisal system examples of documenting behavior, sample action plans, and the realistic opportunities to improve poor or inadequate performance or to recognize exceptional efforts. Both supervisory and nonsupervisory examples and a range of behaviors typical of library employees are included. Though the employees in the case studies are fictitious, their actions and behaviors are composites representing real-life situations.

New Employee

Margot
Circulation/Shelving Clerk

The performance appraisal document is an ideal coaching tool. It is based on observable and documented daily performance. The supervisor documents behaviors or actions that illustrate the employee's need for improvement. Since the supervisor is documenting on-the-job behaviors, and meets with an employee on an "as-needed" basis if a problem arises, there is sufficient opportunity for the employee to reach "meets standards" in the areas of concern by the end of the appraisal period. By having actual examples drawn from the employee's daily interactions with his or her coworkers and with the library's customers, the supervisor is prepared to help the employee improve.

Continuing Patterns of Behavior

When using the performance appraisal document for the annual evaluation process, it is vital to remember that effective evaluation is based on an employee's continuing pattern of behavior. Evaluation for any standard of performance is not based on single, unrelated actions; rather, it is ongoing. When a supervisor perceives that an employee is having difficulty meeting a standard of performance, the supervisor is obligated to discuss with the employee what action is needed to meet that standard. The supervisor and the employee decide on the time and resources available to the employee.

Coaching a New Employee

When using the performance document to coach a new employee, it is not wise to wait too long to correct evident problems. The continuing pattern of behavior can be based on far fewer situations, since a decision on the continuing employment of the new employee usually cannot wait. The new employee, once aware of areas of concern, should have ample opportunity to correct any problems through action plans outlined in the document before a final decision on the continuing employment of that person is made.

Example of a Coaching Review

Following is a description of a new employee in circulation and shelving services, Margot. The job description for her position is also included. The performance appraisal document that follows identifies the changes in behavior that Margot must make to meet the standards of performance set by the library. Margot's supervisor uses the document as the framework for a discussion with her. This coaching review helps the supervisor determine Margot's willingness and ability to change some of her unsatisfactory behaviors. If Margot does improve her performance, she will enhance the delivery of quality service. If she does not improve, her continuing employment at this library is questionable.

Margot

The Hiring

Margot was hired by the library director and the head of circulation and shelving services to fill a part-time circulation and shelving position consisting of weekend and evening hours. It was a difficult position to fill because of the hours required (5 to 9 p.m. and every Saturday). Of the twenty applicants, only five were qualified. Of those five, the director and the head of circulation agreed on Margot, a twenty-four-year-old with an associate's degree in communications.

Margot's experience with customers convinced both the director and the head of circulation and shelving services to hire her. She had worked evening and weekend hours for a major department store in the area. Currently she was working part-time during the day at a local TV station as a "gofer" for the broadcast researchers. (She would pick up documents at locations throughout the city, dig out information at the court house, and input data into the TV station's computer system). She indicated in her interview that she would like to pursue a career in libraries. Her reference from the department store was from her immediate supervisor who stated that Margot had "an obvious interest and liking for people which translated into good sales for her department." Both the director and the head of circulation and shelving services agreed that Margot was friendly, approachable, and intelligent.

The Training

During training, Glenda, the head of circulation and shelving services, noted that Margot learned the computer functions quickly and retained what she knew. She listened to all members of the department without expressing her opinion and did not voice objections about departmental procedures. She was very pleasant to the other members of the department, though she did not personally get involved with them or eat her lunch and have breaks with them. She seemed to seek out the company of supervisors or those staff with advanced degrees. The head of circulation and shelving services observed Margot's interactions with patrons and noted with pleasure that patrons seemed immediately to like Margot; they chatted with her easily about what was going on in their lives. Her work was not only accurate, but compared to several other members of the department, fast and efficient.

Unfortunately, at this point Glenda, the head of circulation and shelving services, had to take her scheduled two-week vacation. Margot had only worked under Glenda's supervision for two weeks; because the hiring process took longer than expected, Glenda did not have as much time supervising Margot before she left as she would have liked. Because of the shortened training period, before she left, Glenda asked the head of adult services and the head of audiovisual services to "help out" if Margot had any questions (there was no assistant supervisor in the department). Glenda did not anticipate any problems since her staff, except for Margot, were experienced and competent.

On-the-Job Behaviors

Upon Glenda's return, she found a tense situation facing her. During her supervisor's absence, Margot exhibited qualities that had not appeared during her interview or training. Margot did work well with patrons, and her work continued to be accurate and fast. However, whenever she finished with her transactions at the circulation desk, and there were no other patrons waiting, she would "wander off" to find other patrons who might be in the popular reading area or in the fiction stacks and engage these patrons in conversation. Some of these conversations were about books the patrons were reading. Not a reader, Margot listened to the patrons, but did not make suggestions for further reading. Neither did she refer the patrons to any member of the popular reading staff.

When a patron did indicate that he was looking for something, Margot would attempt to find the item for him. Again, she did not refer the patron to any other department or staff member. Because of her intelligence, Margot often was able to find what the patron needed. Even when she didn't, the patron went away happy because Margot was so personable and so obviously interested in what the patron had to say. Many times, patrons, especially professional or business people, would give Margot their business cards and suggest she contact them if she needed anything. Sometimes Margot would discuss patrons with other patrons.

For example, she might refer a patron to another patron who was a financial broker or lawyer. Whenever she had free event tickets, which she had received through her work at the TV station, she would hand them out to patrons whom she seemed to think were influential in the community.

Behaviors Affecting Service

Meanwhile, some of the circulation staff were upset because Margot became so interested in her conversations with patrons that she would sometimes neglect to come back to cover the circulation desk. Also, Margot would continually "switch" with other circulation staff so that she could take their front-desk duty and forego her scheduled phone or shelving duties. The circulation staff was becoming increasingly divided about this switching. Those who wanted less front-desk duty were happy, while others viewed the whole situation as unfair. Two of the long-term circulation people did say to Margot that she should be following the regular schedule. Margot listened to them with evident understanding of their concerns, seemed to agree with them, was very pleasant, yet would continue to "switch" whenever she could.

Documenting on-the-Job Behaviors

The head of adult services had observed Margot's actions (and had heard comments from both her own staff and circulation staff) and decided that, in the head of circulation's absence, she would at least say something about Margot's interacting with patrons outside of the circulation department's functions. Again, Margot listened politely and indicated that she understood the head of adult services' concerns. The head of adult services came away from her conversation with Margot with the impression that Margot thought highly of her as a professional whom Margot would like to emulate. Yet Margot continued to do exactly what she had been doing before that conversation. Observing that Margot did not change her behavior, the head of adult services spoke with the head of audiovisual services; they decided to document Margot's actions, but to wait until the head of circulation and shelving services returned and let her deal with Margot.

At this point, the entire staff had become divided. Some staff members liked Margot quite a lot. They thought her energetic, funny, and always willing to listen to their own complaints or gripes. Patrons liked her and asked about her and her work at the TV station. Other staff members criticized her either because she would help patrons with reference work or readers' advisory even though she had not been trained to do so, or because it seemed that "the rules did not apply to her." Some staff members didn't know what to think and had to listen to both sides on breaks or at lunch. Margot was fast becoming *the* hot topic.

Coaching Needed

Upon the head of circulation return, she was immediately bombarded with comments from both Margot's supporters and detractors. After listening to these comments from her staff, Glenda checked with the heads of adult and audiovisual services and received the documentation of Margot's actions during the previous two weeks. After giving Margot's actions some thought, Glenda decided to observe Margot for a week before approaching her about the concerns that had surfaced. Glenda also realized that she had rushed Margot's orientation and training because of the longer than anticipated hiring period and her own scheduled vacation. Glenda had depended upon the heads of adult and audiovisual services to augment Margot's shortened orientation and training. However, that had not worked out the way Glenda had envisioned it might. The more she thought about the situation and the positive comments she also had been receiving from patrons and staff on Margot's approachability, friendliness, and job-specific computer skills, Glenda decided to write up an interim performance appraisal to use with Margot as the structure within which to discuss her specific performance concerns.

Coaching Begins

Using the library's performance document as the framework for discussion, the head of circulation and shelving services coaches Margot on areas needing improvement. The document highlights those standards which Margot currently is not meeting. During the interim review using this document, Glenda and Margot agree on the action plans for the individual standards and the overall actions designed to give Margot the opportunity to meet standards. Margot uses the interim review to express her concerns about the job.

The following performance appraisal document focuses on those standards needing Margot's attention for improvement. (Note that there is no tabulation sheet for a performance rating since this document is not Margot's final evaluation, but rather an interim review to identify areas of concern.)

Her supervisor, Glenda, will be observing Margot's behavior closely during the next few weeks, but also giving her the support she needs to meet the standards (e.g., a more thorough orientation and training review). As indicated on the performance document, Margot and Glenda will sit down for another private review in six weeks to determine whether Margot is improving her performance and what the next step will be.

JOB DESCRIPTION
CIRCULATION/SHELVING CLERK

Position Title	Circulation/Shelving Clerk
Reports to	Head, Circulation/Shelving Services
Category	Clerical
Grade	Level 1 or above
Classification	Part-time, nonexempt or Full-time, nonexempt
Responsibility	To maintain access to the library's materials collections by implementing circulation control procedures and by preserving the physical appearance and order of collections through shelving and shelf-reading.
Duties	*1. Shelve returned informational materials and maintain shelf order in assigned sections.
	*2. Shelf-read assigned sections regularly.
	*3. Sort returned informational items and arrange on shelves and carts for later reshelving.
	*4. Retrieve materials from closed stacks.
	*5. Register new library borrowers and issue borrower cards; update borrower records when appropriate.
	*6. Charge and renew informational items loaned against borrower's record.
	*7. Receive and discharge informational items returned; receive or log fines/fees when appropriate.
	*8. Inspect informational items for damage; follow through with lost and damaged materials' procedures when appropriate.
	*9. Route informational items as received by the library through interlibrary loan or reciprocal borrowing program.
	10. Route informational item reserve requests into circulation control system.
	*11. Notify borrowers of reserved item availability.
	*Indicates essential functions of this position.

12. Prepare notices of overdue informational items and selected circulation-related reports when directed.

13. Answer and route telephone calls as received from the public.

14. Deliver inter-office mail.

*15. Maintain operational status of public service photocopiers; provide appropriate copy change for users.

16. Maintain physical appearance of library by picking up library materials left on tables, counters, chairs, etc.

17. Perform opening and closing duties, including lock-up procedures and floor duty.

18. Perform other related duties as required.

*Indicates essential functions of this position.

Authority   Does not supervise other employees but performs under direct authority of Head, Circulation/Shelving Services.

Experience and Education Required

1. Demonstrated positive support/service attitude is required to meet, communicate with, and serve the public effectively.

2. At the high school graduate level or above, ability to alphabetize, to put numbers in order, and to read and comprehend both written and oral instructions and to respond appropriately is required.

3. Proficiency in the application of basic clerical skills and ability to process information effectively using a computer is required.

4. Pleasant and courteous telephone response is required.

5. Physical strength and dexterity are required to handle informational items and boxes up to 25 pounds in weight, and to transport loaded book carts; physical ability to put items in order on high and low shelves is also required.

PERFORMANCE APPRAISAL

NAME (last, first):	Margot	DATE: 4/20/XX
POSITION:	Circulation/Shelving Clerk	
SUPERVISOR:	Head, Circulation/Shelving Services	
BEGAN EMPLOYMENT:	3/10/XX	

The Standards of Performance system is based on the principle that an employee must know the expectations of the job and that the supervisor will inform the employee of how he or she is performing according to those expectations.

The supervisor will discuss this report with the employee and, if needed, will assist in developing an action plan for improvement.

In signing this report, the employee acknowledges having had the opportunity to review and discuss the performance appraisal, not necessarily that he or she is in agreement with the conclusions.

Upon completion and signature by employee and supervisor, this report is reviewed and signed by the Library Director.

Only the last three annual performance appraisals are kept active for review.

GUIDELINES FOR EVALUATION

- The Code of Service expresses the overall philosophy of service for Rocky River Public Library. The Code is the foundation upon which the Standards of Performance are built.

- The Standards of Performance are the types of behavior expected of an employee necessary to achieve the intent of the Code of Service.

- The Standards of Performance apply to daily performance. Throughout the year the supervisor regularly will evaluate, based on the Standards, the employee's performance.

- Effective evaluation is based on an employee's continuing pattern of behavior. Evaluation for any Standard of Performance is not based on single, unrelated actions.

- Evaluation of an employee is ongoing. When a supervisor perceives that an employee is having difficulty meeting a Standard of Performance, the supervisor is obligated to discuss with the employee what action is needed to meet the standard. The supervisor and the employee decide on the time and resources needed to meet the standard.

- For evaluation, the supervisor must document, with examples of specific, observed actions, any pattern of continuing behavior which either falls into the category of "needs improvement" (NI) or "exceeds standard" (ES). If an employee "meets standard" (MS), the supervisor has the option of either documenting or not.

- In order for an employee to receive an overall "meets standards" or "exceeds standards," the employee must have at least a 2.0 at point B2 on the tabulation sheet. This performance would reflect a level of at least "meets standards" for the employee's position responsibilities.

- Every employee's evaluation is reviewed by the Director, with the option of review by the Deputy Director.

- The employee's compensation is related directly to the employee's evaluation. The overall pattern of the evaluation determines the employee's level of compensation.

- The employee always has both the right and the responsibility to discuss with his or her immediate supervisor any disparity between the employee's interpretation of his or her behavior and the supervisor's interpretation. If the employee and the supervisor cannot come to a mutually agreeable plan of action, the Director is the final arbiter.

PERFORMANCE STANDARDS

A. **Service to Patrons and Coworkers**	
1. *Makes eye contact, greets others sincerely, and speaks in a friendly manner.*	MS

Comments

You have a personable, friendly approach to both patrons and staff. You recognize frequent patrons and carry on pleasant conversations with several patrons.

Examples of Behavior

On several occasions I have observed you in cordial and amicable conversations with patrons.

Action Plan

Maintain and develop your welcoming and professional interactions with patrons within the context of your direct work with them at the circulation desk.

2. *Welcomes and serves without regard to race, color, religion, gender, sexual preference, national origin, disability, age, ancestry, or other characteristics.*	MS

Comments

You exhibit respect for all patrons.

Examples of Behavior

I have not observed you refusing or avoiding serving patrons.

Action Plan

3. *Acknowledges a patron's presence immediately, even if occupied.* NI

   Comments

   On your own initiative, you are frequently away from the front circulation desk with no assigned duties. Once away, you are not aware of lines forming and patrons at circulation needing assistance.

   Examples of Behavior

   I have observed and received comments from other supervisors that you frequently "walk away" from your work station when no patrons are waiting. On several occasions I have observed you being away from your work station when you were not assigned to be so.

   Action Plan

   For the next four weeks, do not leave your work station without supervisory permission.

4. *Does not spend an undue amount of time or effort with one patron if another patron is waiting.* NI

   Comments

   On your own initiative, you are frequently away from the front circulation desk with no assigned duties. Once away, you are not aware of lines forming and patrons at circulation needing assistance.

   Examples of Behavior

   On several occasions I have observed and have had supervisors inform me that you are in conversation with patrons in the fiction stacks when you are assigned to the front circulation desk. On several occasions you were not available to assist patrons at the circulation desk.

   Action Plan

   For the next four weeks, do not leave your work station without supervisory permission. (See also standard A3.)

A.	**Service to Patrons and Coworkers** (continued)	

5. *Takes personal responsibility for meeting patron and staff needs correctly (informational and physical access to materials).* NI

Comments

You do not provide guidance for patrons to the proper department when needed.

Examples of Behavior

On several occasions I or other supervisors have observed you assisting patrons with finding an item. You do not refer the patron to either the reference or popular reading staff when the item is not found.

Action Plan

For the next four weeks, assist patrons only with circulation tasks. Immediately refer reference or readers' advisory questions to the appropriate dept. Review the orientation packet section which describes the differences between reference and assistance questions.

---

6. *Does not communicate any value judgment when interacting with a patron.* ES

Comments

You do not communicate any negative judgment pertaining to any patrons at any time.

Examples of Behavior

I have observed you in conversations with other staff and patrons when another staff member or patron is being discussed. Even when others complain about someone, you do not make any negative comments; you make an attempt to change the focus of the conversation.

Action Plan

7. *Verifies with the patron or coworker that his or her needs have been met.* | NI

Comments

You do not make the effort to verify what your coworkers need, resulting in an increased work load for them.

Examples of Behavior

Your immediate coworkers are the staff at the circulation desk. On numerous occasions, you have not checked with them to see if leaving your station will cause difficulties, which it has (noted: 3/25; 3/27; 3/31; 4/2; 4/5; 4/6).

Action Plan

For the next four weeks, do not leave your work station without supervisory permission. (See also standards A3 and A4.)

8. *Implements appropriate use of technology.* | MS

Comments

In the short period of time you have been with us, you have learned and accurately used the computer functions necessary for your job.

Examples of Behavior

Action Plan

A. **Service to Patrons and Coworkers** (continued)	
9. *Exhibits proper telephone use and etiquette.*	MS
Comments	
You are knowledgeable, responsive, and courteous on the switchboard.	
Examples of Behavior	
Action Plan	
10. *Exhibits a cooperative team spirit.*	NI
Comments	
Frequently, you act independently without considering the work load of your coworkers.	
Examples of Behavior	
You "walk away" from your work station with no assigned duties and stay away without realizing that your coworkers need your help.	
Action Plan	
For the next four weeks, do not leave your work station without supervisory permission. When not busy with patrons, offer your assistance to other staff in the circulation department.	

11. *Puts service above any personal activities or interests while on duty.*

MS

Comments

Be careful that you do not cross the line between being helpful to patrons (handing out free event tickets) and promoting your nonlibrary interests. This line is a fine line—be aware of your actions and the perception of others.

Examples of Behavior

Action Plan

12. *Is ready for duty at/during scheduled times.*

NI

Comments

You frequently are not at your work station when assigned.

Examples of Behavior

See standard A7 for examples.

Action Plan

See action plan under standards A3, A4, A7.

A.	**Service to Patrons and Coworkers** (continued)	
	13. *Is attentive to others' complaints and, when applicable, refers the complaints to the appropriate level.*	MS
	Comments	
	Examples of Behavior	
	Action Plan	
	14. *Takes responsibility for learning updated internal procedures.*	MS
	Comments	
	Examples of Behavior	
	Action Plan	

15. *Upholds library policies and established procedures.*		MS
Comments		
Examples of Behavior		
Action Plan		
16. *Upholds the intellectual freedom of the patron.*		MS
Comments		
Examples of Behavior		
Action Plan		
17. *Upholds all confidentiality rights of the patron.*		MS
Comments		
Examples of Behavior		
Action Plan		

B.	**Personal Development**	
	1. *Plans own time to meet obligations and specified deadlines.*	MS
	Comments	
	Examples of Behavior	
	Action Plan	

	2. *Actively listens to supervisor and accepts direction, seeking further advice from the supervisor as needed.*	NI

Comments

During your training, I emphasized the importance of being at your assigned work station. Also, during my absence, the head of adult services asked you not to attempt to answer reference questions, but to direct patrons to the appropriate department (reference or popular reading).

Examples of Behavior

On numerous occasions, I have observed and other supervisors (head of adult services; head of audiovisual services) have observed you not at your assigned duties (switching duties with other circulation staff; "walking away" from the circulation desk). While away from your work station, you attempt to answer patron questions without referring the patron to the appropriate department.

Action Plan

Follow the direction given to you by a supervisor; ask if you are unsure what you should be doing. Do not switch duties with any other coworker. Stay at your work station unless you are reassigned by me or another supervisor.

3. *Accepts responsibility for own actions and obligations.*	MS
Comments	
Examples of Behavior	
Action Plan	
4. *Adapts to change.*	MS
Comments	
Examples of Behavior	
Action Plan	

B.	**Personal Development** (continued)	
	5. *Uses library-provided means for continuing education or training.*	MS
	Comments	
	Examples of Behavior	
	Action Plan	

	6. *Communicates clearly and honestly.*	NI
	Comments	
	You are often uncommunicative with supervisors and coworkers.	
	Examples of Behavior	
	You listen to others, but your actions indicate that you do not respond to their concerns. During your training, I instructed you on your duties, informing you of the importance of being ready to assist patrons at the circulation desk. In my absence, both the head of adult services and the head of audiovisual services spoke with you about remaining at your work station. You disregarded their instruction.	
	Action Plan	
	When instructed by me or another supervisor, verify the direction you are being given by repeating the instructions back to the supervisor. If you do not clearly undestand what is expected of you, ask.	

7. *Demonstrates appropriate initiative within a team framework.*   NI

    Comments

    When you finish your assigned duties, you leave your work station without checking with me or another supervisor.

    Examples of Behavior

    See standards A3, A4, and A7.

    Action Plan

    Follow action plans under standards A3, A4, A7.

C.	**Specific Job Standards**	
	Items under this category relate directly to the individual's position description.	
	1. Provides user's first contact point upon entry to the building.	MS
	Comments	
	You present a welcoming, customer-friendly first contact with the public.	
	Examples of Behavior	
	Action Plan	
	2. Sorts, shelves, and shelf-reads the collections (adult, juvenile, young adult, periodicals, and audiovisual).	MS
	Comments	
	Your sorting, shelving, and shelf-reading is accurate and efficient.	
	Examples of Behavior	
	Action Plan	

Items under this category relate directly to the individual's position description.

3. Charges, renews, and discharges informational items. Enters new registrations. Provides clear and accurate information to patrons about fines, overdues, and items on loan.

MS

Comments

You are knowledgeable and accurate when using the automated circulation system. You clearly communicate with patrons about the activity on their borrowing records.

Examples of Behavior

Action Plan

4. Implements reserve system. Enters holds and makes reserve calls.

MS

Comments

Examples of Behavior

Action Plan

C.	**Specific Job Standards** (continued)	
	Items under this category relate directly to the individual's position description.	
	5. Answers incoming calls and directs callers appropriately.	MS
	Comments	
	You are knowledgeable about telephone operations. You efficiently answer and accurately transfer incoming calls.	
	Examples of Behavior	
	Action Plan	

Comments by Supervisor

After an unexpectedly shortened training period, you have learned the functions of the automated circulation system and performed them accurately and efficiently. You welcome patrons in a friendly manner, putting them instantly at ease.

As noted during this interim performance review, you are disrupting service to the public by not being available at your work station as assigned. The examples cited illustrate that quality service is not being given because you are not at your work station to assist when needed; lines of waiting patrons develop and coworkers are rushed to keep up with the demand.

Because I feel you have valuable strengths that add to service in our department (making patrons feel welcome and at ease and your quick learning and retention of circulation tasks), and because I was not able to spend as much time with you during the training period as I had originally planned, I am suggesting the action plan outlined below as a means for you to improve your performance and meet standards.

Overall Action Plan

Follow the action plans outlined in this performance document. As supervisor, I will continue your training period for an additional two weeks. You and I will also review the parts of the orientation package that explain the various functions of each department and the ways in which each department supports the others. On your own, you will review the policy manual. You will ask me about any areas about which you are unfamiliar or unsure. I will observe your actions and inform you of any actions that do not meet standards. Six weeks from today, we will meet to review progress made on meeting the standards. If substantial progress has not been made on meeting the standards, your continued employment at this library is in jeopardy.

_____
Employee's signature   Date

_____
Supervisor's signature   Date

_____
Reviewer's signature   Date

Recommended for Level: _____

Comments by Employee

I enjoy working here and will strive to meet the standards for which my supervisor says I need improvement. I will note, however, that the only reason I leave my work station is that I am bored when there are no customers waiting. I am used to a constant, high level of activity in my other jobs. I do understand that when I am away, I am not aware when the desk gets busy. I'll follow the action plans outlined with the hope that after I meet standards, I will be given the opportunity to take on increased responsibilities so I do not get bored so easily.

_____

Employee's signature   Date

_____

Supervisor's signature   Date

_____

Reviewer's signature   Date

CASE STUDY

Long-Term Employee

Eleanore
Circulation/Shelving Clerk

P erformance appraisal of long-term employees sometimes can be frustrating for both the employee and the supervisor. An employee may feel unappreciated if he or she automatically receives the same performance rating year after year merely because of the "invisibility factor." This invisibility factor results from the employee doing the same job over a long period of time with his or her performance set in stone in the supervisor's mind, and with little or no hope of change. Over time, the employee loses any interest in excelling, since he or she feels there is no hope of recognition.

If a supervisor has no reason to look closely at individual behaviors that enhance quality service, the employee is rated on longevity rather than any contributions to—or distractions from—the delivery of excellent service. The long-term employee loses incentive to look beyond what he or she is doing daily. Possibly valuable skills remain underused.

Library-wide Criteria

In this performance appraisal system, focus is on behaviors or actions that the library has determined are vital to the library's Code of Service. Any employee, whether new or long-term, is evaluated on the same library-wide criteria. All employees have an equal and fair opportunity to meet or exceed a standard. A long-term employee can seize opportunities to excel and, in the process, be revitalized.

Using the standards and guidelines, a supervisor can suggest ways in which a long-term employee can contribute—perhaps through a special project, assisting the supervisor in training new employees, or a regular program of offering ideas for improving service in the department. The choice of accepting the challenge is up to the long-term employee. However, at least the choice, with recognition, is present.

Eleanore

The Hiring

Eleanore is a long-time employee of the library. She started with the library when it was still a small public library with a staff of fifteen and limited open hours. Eleanore was hired as a part-time shelver, a few hours a week. In her early forties, and unexpectedly widowed, she was looking for a place to interact with people. Because she had an income from her husband's insurance, she did not need to support herself and was not interested in starting a career.

On-the-Job Learning

When hired, Eleanore had a high school education and no library experience (or any working experience, for that matter). However, because the library was woefully understaffed "way back when," and the children's, adult, and circulation departments and stacks were on one floor within sight of each other, Eleanore would step in wherever needed—checking out books, helping a parent find a picture book, or picking out a good mystery book for an older patron to read. Basically, she learned how to help people in all the public service departments through observing the library's one professionally trained librarian (the head librarian) and the other employees. She was a quick learner; in a quiet, obliging manner, she helped out whenever she could.

Eleanore enjoyed her work: the variety; the rapport with the other staff who not only got along well at work, but who also occasionally socialized together; and most especially, the number of very nice patrons she grew to know over the years.

Gradually, Eleanore's hours increased until she was hired as a full-time employee in the circulation department. At this point, she had already remarried. She really did not have to work, but she had become so attached to the library and its patrons that she could not conceive of leaving. The size of the library and its collections, and the limited staff, still required Eleanore to "fill in" for other positions as needed.

The Change

About ten years after Eleanore joined the library staff, the head librarian retired and was replaced by an energetic director who added additional services to attract more users of the library. Charismatic and outgoing, this director was also able to increase funding enough to expand the library. Over an eight-year period, the square footage of the building doubled and the number of staff increased to forty. The educational requirements for the various positions were enhanced. As professionally trained librarians were hired and given the resources of time and money, the library began to offer specific services tailored to community needs.

A professional outreach librarian was hired to serve homebound patrons, the retirement home, and the nursing home. A business librarian met the needs of the local businesses through programs, electronic business resources, and a relevant circulating collection. A young adult librarian developed a relationship with the schools so the library would have the information needed for curriculum support of public and private school reports and the increasing number of home schoolers. Both the adult and children's departments finally were adequately staffed so that time could be spent doing long-neglected collection development.

Declining Motivation

This evolutionary period was very exciting—but also very exhausting for the employees who had been part of the library before its explosive growth. Eleanore was one of the fortunate ones. Because she cared deeply about the library, its staff, and the people she had always served, she was motivated to stay throughout all the changes. And she truly did believe that, though difficult for the staff, the changes in the library were good. As more and more people used the library, the library's reputation grew, and Eleanore was proud of the work that the staff accomplished. Though staff no longer socialized outside work, they still worked well together.

Eleanore continued to enjoy working with most of the staff and had very good rapport with the patrons. Eleanore's graciousness and the skills she had learned over the years when working with a wide variety of people served her well as the number and types of patrons continued to grow.

The down side for Eleanore was that, as more professional librarians were hired, and the job duties became more specialized, she no longer could "fill in" for staff in other departments. Though Eleanore still enjoyed her interactions with the public, she was beginning to tire of the specific circulation duties, which did not vary much from day to day. With the growth of the library, the circulation department had become busier and busier; however, its basic tasks—registering borrowers, checking out and checking in materials, sorting items for shelving—had not changed significantly. As different formats were added to the collections (first compact discs, then videocassettes), procedures also changed. However, Eleanore did not have the opportunity to participate in any of the decisions on how the department was being run. Frankly, she was getting bored.

This situation continued for the next two years. Eleanore knew that the library soon would be automating, with the circulation functions being the first. At this point, Eleanore was not sure she wanted to experience any more change. In fact, she was not feeling very good about herself or her job. The library was busy, but she had been doing the same things the same way for so long, she was just plain tired. Though her husband was encouraging her to quit, he also was traveling more for his work, and Eleanore was not sure she wanted to adjust to being alone at home.

Emphasis
on Staff Improvement

Fortunately, at the same time Eleanore was experiencing the lack of motivation and the beginnings of inertia that come with long-term employment, the charismatic director looked at the internal state of the library and recognized the critical need for staff development. The financial resources of the library now permitted the hiring of an assistant director whose responsibilities included spearheading the development of an effective performance appraisal system, providing training in supervisory skills (including active listening, coaching, team building) and working with various departments to cultivate opportunities for staff growth.

Over a two-year period, there were significant signs that the emphasis on staff development was producing desired results. Staff were actively encouraged to participate in the decision-making processes within the departments. Though the organization was not yet at a stage where opportunities for growth were plentiful, the atmosphere had changed just enough that a thoughtful employee could find chances to contribute in new ways.

Eleanore's Opportunity

After much contemplation and weighing of her options (quit and stay home; quit and find other employment; stay bored in her current position), Eleanore decided to see if she could find a way to replicate that experience of variety which she so enjoyed when she first started at the library. In small ways, she began to offer suggestions within her department. Many of her suggestions centered around recognizing the fear of technology that many of the older patrons were expressing. During the check-out process, Eleanore would often hear comments from the long-time patrons about how much they were dreading the impending "computer catalog." Eleanore heard lamentations (often jokingly expressed, but real nonetheless) over the loss of the paper card catalog.

When Eleanore voiced these concerns to her supervisor, she was asked to join the library-wide staff group that was responsible for the automation project. Eleanore brought not only the older person's perspective, but also, from her earlier days at the library, the valuable knowledge of how all the departments interact and depend on one another. Eleanore's basic job duties did not change. However, the experience of serving on the automation team revitalized her and opened her mind to thinking of other ways in which she could support the library she loved so much.

Her performance evaluation reflects the ways she excels in areas that fall outside her normal job duties. It illustrates how a long-term employee, using the experience gained during a long tenure, can seize opportunities outside his or her regular job duties to develop and grow professionally.

CIRCULATION/SHELVING CLERK

Position Title	Circulation/Shelving Clerk
Reports to	Head, Circulation/Shelving Services
Category	Clerical
Grade	Level 1 or above
Classification	Part-time, nonexempt or Full-time, nonexempt
Responsibility	To maintain access to the library's materials collections by implementing circulation control procedures and by preserving the physical appearance and order of collections through shelving and shelf-reading.
Duties	

*1. Shelve returned informational materials and maintain shelf order in assigned sections.

*2. Shelf-read assigned sections regularly.

*3. Sort returned informational items and arrange on shelves and carts for later reshelving.

*4. Retrieve materials from closed stacks.

*5. Register new library borrowers and issue borrower cards; update borrower records when appropriate.

*6. Charge and renew informational items loaned against borrower's record.

*7. Receive and discharge informational items returned; receive or log fines/fees when appropriate.

*8. Inspect informational items for damage; follow through with lost and damaged materials' procedures when appropriate.

*9. Route informational items as received by the library through interlibrary loan or reciprocal borrowing program.

10. Route informational item reserve requests into circulation control system.

*11. Notify borrowers of reserved item availability.

*Indicates essential functions of this position.

12. Prepare notices of overdue informational items and selected circulation-related reports when directed.

13. Answer and route telephone calls as received from the public.

14. Deliver inter-office mail.

*15. Maintain operational status of public service photocopiers; provide appropriate copy change for users.

16. Maintain physical appearance of library by picking up library materials left on tables, counters, chairs, etc.

17. Perform opening and closing duties, including lock up procedures and floor duty.

18. Perform other related duties as required.

*Indicates essential functions of this position.

Authority   Does not supervise other employees but performs under direct authority of Head, Circulation/Shelving Services.

Experience and Education Required

1. Demonstrated positive support/service attitude is required to meet, communicate with, and serve the public effectively.

2. At the high school graduate level or above, ability to alphabetize, to put numbers in order, and to read and comprehend both written and oral instructions and to respond appropriately is required.

3. Proficiency in the application of basic clerical skills and ability to process information effectively using a computer is required.

4. Pleasant and courteous telephone response is required.

5. Physical strength and dexterity are required to handle informational items and boxes up to 25 pounds in weight, and to transport loaded book carts; physical ability to put items in order on high and low shelves is also required.

PERFORMANCE APPRAISAL

NAME (last, first):	Eleanore	DATE: 11/10/XX
POSITION:	Circulation/Shelving Clerk	
SUPERVISOR:	Head, Circulation/Shelving Services	
BEGAN EMPLOYMENT:	6/5/XX	

The Standards of Performance system is based on the principle that an employee must know the expectations of the job and that the supervisor will inform the employee of how he or she is performing according to those expectations.

The supervisor will discuss this report with the employee and, if needed, will assist in developing an action plan for improvement.

In signing this report, the employee acknowledges having had the opportunity to review and discuss the performance appraisal, not necessarily that he or she is in agreement with the conclusions.

Upon completion and signature by employee and supervisor, this report is reviewed and signed by the Library Director.

Only the last three annual performance appraisals are kept active for review.

GUIDELINES FOR EVALUATION

- The Code of Service expresses the overall philosophy of service for Rocky River Public Library. The Code is the foundation upon which the Standards of Performance are built.

- The Standards of Performance are the types of behavior expected of an employee necessary to achieve the intent of the Code of Service.

- The Standards of Performance apply to daily performance. Throughout the year the supervisor regularly will evaluate, based on the Standards, the employee's performance.

- Effective evaluation is based on an employee's continuing pattern of behavior. Evaluation for any Standard of Performance is not based on single, unrelated actions.

- Evaluation of an employee is ongoing. When a supervisor perceives that an employee is having difficulty meeting a Standard of Performance, the supervisor is obligated to discuss with the employee what action is needed to meet the standard. The supervisor and the employee decide on the time and resources needed to meet the standard.

- For evaluation, the supervisor must document, with examples of specific, observed actions, any pattern of continuing behavior which either falls into the category of "needs improvement" (NI) or "exceeds standard" (ES). If an employee "meets standard" (MS), the supervisor has the option of either documenting or not.

- In order for an employee to receive an overall "meets standards" or "exceeds standards," the employee must have at least a 2.0 at point B2 on the tabulation sheet. This performance would reflect a level of at least "meets standards" for the employee's position responsibilities.

- Every employee's evaluation is reviewed by the Director, with the option of review by the Deputy Director.

- The employee's compensation is related directly to the employee's evaluation. The overall pattern of the evaluation determines the employee's level of compensation.

- The employee always has both the right and the responsibility to discuss with his or her immediate supervisor any disparity between the employee's interpretation of his or her behavior and the supervisor's interpretation. If the employee and the supervisor cannot come to a mutually agreeable plan of action, the Director is the final arbiter.

PERFORMANCE STANDARDS

A.	**Service to Patrons and Coworkers**	

1. *Makes eye contact, greets others sincerely, and speaks in a friendly manner.*

ES

Comments

You are able to carry on a friendly conversation with most of the patrons with whom you have contact.

Examples of Behavior

You consistently know by name the patrons you serve—not only the long-time patrons whom you have known for many years, but also more recent patrons. On numerous occasions I have observed you carry on a friendly conversation with new borrowers. Consistently, you make our patrons feel welcomed.

Action Plan

---

2. *Welcomes and serves without regard to race, color, religion, gender, sexual preference, national origin, disability, age, ancestry, or other characteristics.*

MS

Comments

You welcome and serve all patrons equally.

Examples of Behavior

Action Plan

3. *Acknowledges a patron's presence immediately, even if occupied.*

MS

Comments

You gracefully and quickly end your conversation with a patron if another patron approaches.

Examples of Behavior

Action Plan

4. *Does not spend an undue amount of time or effort with one patron if another patron is waiting.*

MS

Comments

Examples of Behavior

Action Plan

A.	**Service to Patrons and Coworkers** (continued)	
	5. *Takes personal responsibility for meeting patron and staff needs correctly (informational and physical access to materials).*	MS
	Comments	
	Through your previous experiences in "helping out" in other departments, you are able to answer general questions relating to both adult and children's areas.	
	Examples of Behavior	
	Action Plan	
	6. *Does not communicate any value judgment when interacting with a patron.*	ES
	Comments	
	You do not communicate any negative judgment pertaining to any patrons at any time.	
	Examples of Behavior	
	I have never observed you commenting in a negative manner about any patron. In fact, on several occasions, I have noted that you skillfully will turn a conversation with a coworker away from complaints about a patron.	
	Action Plan	

7. *Verifies with the patron or coworker that his or her needs have been met.*

   MS

   Comments

   Examples of Behavior

   Action Plan

8. *Implements appropriate use of technology.*

   ES

   Comments

   As part of the library-wide automation team, you have become a resource person for other staff to learn about how technology affects the older person's use of the library.

   Examples of Behavior

   From the minutes and reports of the automation team, and from the automation team's presentations at staff training sessions, I know that you have offered valuable guidelines for integrating technology into the daily public use of the library. You have helped design classes to encourage patron use of the automated card catalog. You have assisted me in training our department's staff in using the automated catalog. Your steady, practical example of learning new technology has been a model for our department's staff to follow.

   Action Plan

A.	**Service to Patrons and Coworkers** (continued)	
	9. *Exhibits proper telephone use and etiquette.*	ES

Comments

Your exemplary personal skills with patrons transfers to your telephone and switchboard duties as well.

Examples of Behavior

I use you to help train new staff on the proper operation of the telephone. You have offered suggestions and designed handy "cheat sheets," to aid staff in knowing where to transfer calls. Without being asked, you have helped staff in other departments distinguish between intercom and transferred calls (per adult and children's supervisors).

Action Plan

	10. *Exhibits a cooperative team spirit.*	ES

Comments

Your work with the automation team has showcased your ability to promote cooperation among staff with differing work styles and abilities.

Examples of Behavior

On many occasions, your unruffled manner and strong belief in the mission of the library has eased the strain and stress associated with our library's automation project. On both an individual and a group basis, you have provided valued support during automation training. You also step in to help staff with disgruntled patrons who are expressing frustration with the new automated catalog. Your coworkers have expressed to me their appreciation for your tactful and thoughtful help (e.g., e-mail messages of March, April, June, and October).

Action Plan

11. *Puts service above any personal activities or interests while on duty.*	MS
Comments	
Examples of Behavior	
Action Plan	
12. *Is ready for duty at/during scheduled times.*	MS
Comments	
Examples of Behavior	
Action Plan	

A.	**Service to Patrons and Coworkers** (continued)	
	13. *Is attentive to others' complaints and, when applicable, refers the complaints to the appropriate level.*	ES
	Comments	
	You alerted first me, then the administration, of the genuine fears of both patrons and staff over the impending automation of the library.	
	Examples of Behavior	
	You expressed your concerns first to me, your supervisor, and then, with my support, to the administration. You not only expressed the concerns, but had thought about possible remedies for the fear. You offered suggestions for dealing with the complaints. Several of your suggestions are being implemented, including a brochure/handout to explain in simple terms the automation process and timetable.	
	Action Plan	
	14. *Takes responsibility for learning updated internal procedures.*	ES
	Comments	
	You are actively involved in the development of automation training.	
	Examples of Behavior	
	Your ideas for both staff and patron automation training have been or are in the process of being implemented (e.g., small classes both in the library and at the Senior Center, the retirement home, and sessions offered by you at "Grandparents' Day" at the Intermediate School). You assist me in training our department's staff (e.g., our monthly training sessions).	
	Action Plan	

15. *Upholds library policies and established procedures.* MS

Comments

Examples of Behavior

Action Plan

16. *Upholds the intellectual freedom of the patron.* MS

Comments

Examples of Behavior

Action Plan

A.	**Service to Patrons and Coworkers** (continued)	
	17. *Upholds all confidentiality rights of the patron.*	MS
	Comments	
	Examples of Behavior	
	Action Plan	

B.	**Personal Development**	
	1. *Plans own time to meet obligations and specified deadlines.*	MS
	Comments	
	Examples of Behavior	
	Action Plan	
	2. *Actively listens to supervisor and accepts direction, seeking further advice from the supervisor as needed.*	MS
	Comments	
	Examples of Behavior	
	Action Plan	

B.	**Personal Development** (continued)	
	3. *Accepts responsibility for own actions and obligations.*	MS
	Comments	
	Examples of Behavior	
	Action Plan	
	4. *Adapts to change.*	ES
	Comments	
	You actively assist both patrons and staff with changes that affect them.	
	Examples of Behavior	
	You have been and continue to be a strong supporter and advocate of the library-wide automation project which affects all aspects of library service. You are involved in ongoing training of both patrons and staff. You offer explanations of the benefits of the change to both individuals and at meetings of community groups (the garden clubs, the Rotary, residents of the retirement home, PTAs, etc.).	
	Action Plan	

5. *Uses library-provided means for continuing education or training.* MS

Comments

I encourage you to enhance the training skills you learned during this automation project by attending specific workshops on training given by our state library association. You have the potential to become a valuable trainer!

Examples of Behavior

Action Plan

6. *Communicates clearly and honestly.* MS

Comments

Examples of Behavior

Action Plan

B.	**Personal Development** (continued)	
	7. *Demonstrates appropriate initiative within a team framework.*	ES

Comments

You have offered workable ways to improve service.

Examples of Behavior

Because of your suggestions, we have been able to simplify procedures, resulting in faster and better service for our patrons. For example, you suggested we eliminate the check-in step for the new book cart since Technical Service already does that before sending the cart up; we are following your suggestion to put the phone number of the patron on the request slip, making the process of calling a patron with a reserve much faster; you initiated the short "morning review" of shortcuts in the automated check-in and check-out functions, resulting in more effective training for our department.

Action Plan

C. **Specific Job Standards**

Items under this category relate directly to the individual's position description.

1. Provides user's first contact point upon entry to the building.   ES

   Comments

   You are consistently welcoming to our patrons; you serve all equally in a very positive, pleasant manner. You know most of our patrons by name or well enough to carry on a friendly conversation with them.

   Examples of Behavior

   On numerous occasions I have received many compliments about you from our patrons (see file). Patrons know you by name and will go to you for check-out if given a choice.

   Action Plan

2. Sorts, shelves, and shelf-reads the collections (adult, juvenile, young adult, periodicals, and audiovisual).   MS

   Comments

   Your work is accurate and efficient.

   Examples of Behavior

   Action Plan

C. **Specific Job Standards** (continued) *Items under this category relate directly to the individual's position description.*	
3. Charges, renews, and discharges informational items. Enters new registrations. Provides clear and accurate information to patrons about fines, overdues, and items on loan.	MS
Comments Your work is accurate and efficient. *Examples of Behavior* *Action Plan*	
4. Implements reserve system. Enters holds and makes reserve calls.	MS
Comments *Examples of Behavior* *Action Plan*	

Items under this category relate directly to the individual's position description.

5. Answers incoming calls and directs callers appropriately.　　ES

   Comments

   Your knowledge of telephone operation, and the courtesy and efficiency you exhibit when assigned switchboard duties, provide an exemplary standard for other staff.

   Examples of Behavior

   This year you have trained three new staff members for switchboard duties. You have also provided helpful shortcuts and handy written tips not only for our department, but for adult and children's services staff as well.

   Action Plan

Comments by Supervisor

Your initiative in recognizing the need for educating and training those patrons (and staff) who are cautious about the automated catalog is much appreciated. Your "early alert" to potential public relations problems surrounding the automation project and your thoughtful suggestions for diffusing complaints have greatly contributed to a smooth transition to an automated circulation system. Your knowledge of how the library operations interrelate, coupled with your caring behavior towards both patrons and staff, has enhanced the service of our department. I encourage you to attend training workshops offered by our cooperative library system. You have a true knack for helping people see the benefits of doing something differently! A goal for next year is to attend at least one training workshop and to incorporate two new training techniques with staff in our department.

Overall Action Plan

_____

Employee's signature   Date

_____

Supervisor's signature   Date

_____

Reviewer's signature   Date

Recommended for Level: _____

Comments by Employee

I appreciate the opportunity to "grow" in my job through working with the automation team. I am enjoying my work. The staff is great, and I am having fun talking to community groups. Thanks!

_____

Employee's signature   Date

_____

Supervisor's signature   Date

_____

Reviewer's signature   Date

STANDARDS OF PERFORMANCE
TABULATION SHEET

ES = 3 points; MS = 2 points; NI = 1 point
Round all numbers to the nearest "tenth" at each step of the calculation
(except B2)—Examples: 2.41 = 2.4 and 2.75 = 2.8.

1. Determine the total number of applicable standards for each:

   Service: _17_
   Personal Development: _7_

          Total above two categories: _24_ (A)

   Specific Job Standards: _5_
   Supervisory: _0_

          Total above two categories: _5_ (B)

2. Determine point value for each of the applicable sections:

   Service:
   number of ES X 3 = _21_ number of MS X 2 = _20_ number of NI = _0_
          Total for Service Standards: _41_

   Personal Development:
   number of ES X 3 = _6_ number of MS X 2 = _10_ number of NI = _0_
          Total for Personal Development: _16_

          Grand total of above two categories: _57_ (A1)

   Specific Job Standards:
   number of ES X 3 = _6_ number of MS X 2 = _6_ number of NI = _0_
          Total for Specific Job Standards: _12_

   Supervisory:
   number of ES X 3 = _0_ number of MS X 2 = _0_ number of NI = _0_
          Total for Supervisory Standards: _0_

          Grand total of above two categories: _12_ (B1)

3. To determine the overall point value for Service and Development sections:

    Take **A1** *57* and divide by **A** *24*

    This results in **A2:** *2.4* (the value for these sections)

4. To determine overall point value for the specific Job Standards and Supervisors:

    Take **B1** *12* and divide by **B** *5*

    This results in **B2:** *2.4* * (the value for these sections)

    > *** B2:**
    > **Must be 2.0 or higher to proceed with calculation.**

5. To determine overall point value for this evaluation:

    Add **A2** *2.4* to **B2** *2.4* This results in **B3:** *4.8*

    Now divide **B3** by 2 *2.4* This is the total point value for this evaluation

    Using this number, the **overall evaluation** is rated *MS3*

ES	= 2.5 or higher
MS3	= 2.4–2.2
MS2	= 2.1–1.8
MS1	= 1.7–1.5
NI	= 1.4 or lower

Employee's name: _____

Supervisor's signature:_____

Date: _____

Supervisory Employee

Holly
Head, Children's Services

In small and medium-sized libraries, a supervisor is often someone who has specific job duties as well as responsibility for supervising a departmental staff. For example, the head of outreach services supervises employees who deliver books to the homebound, rotate satellite collections in the community, drive the bookmobile, and present programs. Yet this supervisor is also a librarian who spends part of her or his time providing direct public service (handling information requests and circulation) on the bookmobile. The head of technical services supervises staff who order and process library materials, but he or she is also required to catalog items daily.

Supervisory Job Duties

In the Performance Appraisal document (Appendix D), section C: Specific Job Standards relates to the nonsupervisory duties of the supervisor—either the direct contact with the public (e.g., information or circulation services) or the indirect support (e.g., cataloging, business office, maintenance services) needed for effective library operation. Section D: Supervisory Standards relates to the way the supervisor manages his or her staff. This section sets the library-wide standards for supervision. No matter what the specific job duties of the supervisor, he or she is expected, for example, to "effectively and fairly manage resources" (standard D6) and "actively coordinate with other departments" (standard D9). For the supervisor's end-of-appraisal-year evaluation, sections C and D are combined for the "job" portion of the evaluation.

Supervisory Standards

The Standards of Performance Guidelines document (Appendix B) gives examples of behaviors for meeting the Supervisory Standards. The same as for the other standards, these guidelines indicate the levels of behavior for "meets," "exceeds," or "needs improvement." For a supervisor, the examples of behavior are often closely tied to library-wide, as well as departmental, projects or goals. A supervisor may well be part of a library management team or assigned to lead a special project affecting other departments or overall library service. The examples of behavior for "exceeds standard" or "needs improvement" reflect that high level of responsibility.

The Supervisory Standards ensure that all supervisors know the expectations the library has for the delivery of quality service. In addition, staff members realize that the library expects a high standard of management from all supervisors.

Holly

Background

Holly has been head of children's services for three years. Before being hired as head, she had been a children's librarian at a larger library for four years (one year as a paraprofessional and three years with her MLS). When she was chosen as the new head of children's services, she was very excited about implementing her ideas for meeting the needs of the children of the community. She and her staff serve children from preschoolers through the sixth grade and their parents; they also provide curriculum support for school assignments.

The First Year

Holly's enthusiasm and drive did not diminish during her first year as supervisor of the department, even though she soon discovered upon her arrival that the children's services staff were demoralized and did not exhibit the energy she was hoping they would have. The former head of the department had been very controlling and autocratic. She had not shared the storytelling with the other two librarians; she also did all the ordering of titles for the collection. Basically, the two librarians helped the children with informational questions after school and evenings, but did not participate in any programming and collection management duties. Consequently, service suffered since those major responsibilities rested with only one person, and the abilities of the other children's services staff were vastly underused. Before Holly arrived, the atmosphere in the children's department was one of restraint and lackluster service.

Fortunately, Holly immediately sat down with her staff and outlined what she expected—full participation in planning and conducting story times, in reading reviews, and in recommending titles for the collections. She presented her philosophy of service—the highest quality of service for all users of the library and a team effort to achieve that goal.

Supervisory Standards in Action

Holly used the performance appraisal document to coach her staff on improving performance. After helping her staff recognize and practice skills they had not previously used, she delegated responsibilities to gain the time and resources to expand services. It took her a full year to get the department at what she considered a minimum level of service.

That first year truly tested Holly's skills in not only motivating staff, but also in managing her budget to revitalize the juvenile collections. Additionally, during that first year, she learned how the children's services' goals fit into the library's long-term plan, a knowledge that helped her in the succeeding years seek increased funding for expanded programming, collections, and services.

Persuasive, tactful, and energetic, Holly generated excitement for children's services within both the library and the community. She made valuable contacts, not only with the school librarians, but also the principals of both the public and the one private school in the community. She encouraged class visits and promoted examples of library/school cooperation with the local newspaper and the PTAs. She built upon the good publicity her department received by asking the PTA groups to sponsor special events for the various age groups. The Intermediate School PTA donated money for a popular magician event in the library, and the Primary School PTA funded a national storyteller who attracted many parents and their children who previously had not used the library.

Growth Within the Department

Holly's outgoing, pleasant style and genuine interest in helping children discover the library helped her forge enduring relationships with many of the parents and families. Soon, the parents and children felt very welcome in the library and sought out Holly to just say "hello!" Many influential members of the community now brought in their children for story times. When they asked about additional sessions (since the story times filled up so quickly), Holly was quick to point out the need for more funds for expanded staff and services.

Holly and her staff focused on finding out what the community wanted in children's services—and then delivered, as resources would permit, as much as they could. *How* they delivered those services is what won the hearts of many of the families who used the library.

Over the following two years, two new librarians and a clerk were hired to support the increased activity in the department which included more story times, a juvenile outreach program to day care centers and nurseries, joint programming efforts with the primary school PTAs, and the introduction of an "after-school" computer lab with CD-ROM databases and Internet access.

Supervisory Growth

Throughout these years of growth, Holly coordinated activities with the supervisors of other departments and built a solid reputation for cooperation and creativity. As her knowledge of the strengths and skills of the people she worked with grew, her abilities became more evident. As part of the library's management team, she contributed ideas and plans for enhancing overall library service, especially in the implementation of technology in the library. Active in the community, she successfully helped to solicit funds for new computer workstations and technology training.

Her end-of-appraisal-year evaluation for her third full year with the library recognizes the high quality of service her supervision of a busy, productive department continues to provide.

JOB DESCRIPTION
HEAD, CHILDREN'S SERVICES

Position Title	Head, Children's Services
Reports to	Assistant Director
Category	Professional
Grade	Level 1 or above
Classification	Full-time, exempt
Responsibility	To provide strong, creative departmental supervisory leadership to assure the effectiveness and appropriateness of the juvenile information collections and the delivery of a diverse and relevant schedule of programming through the sixth grade level.

Duties

*1. Coordinate all departmental activities as supervisor by training, monitoring, and scheduling all departmental staff.

*2. Coordinate collection development of all juvenile reference and circulating materials. Maintain budgetary and overview responsibilities for these collections but delegate actual collection management duties to staff trained in approved techniques for acquisition, evaluation, weeding, and inventory of the collections.

*3. Coordinate through planning and evaluation the delivery of a diverse and relevant schedule of programming events for children from birth through grade six.

*4. Evaluate all departmental staff by using the library-wide standards of the approved performance appraisal system.

*5. Identify, evaluate, and implement appropriate service enhancements to continually improve the effective and efficient delivery of services to children.

*6. Provide direct informational, readers' advisory, and programming service to the users of Children's Services.

*7. Demonstrate leadership through departmental staff meetings, through design and support of staff training opportunities, and through effective communication.

*8. Participate in the interviewing and selection of all departmental staff.

9. Participate in community and professional activities directly related to Children's Services.

*Indicates essential functions of this position.

10. Promote awareness of the activities of Children's Services.

11. Perform other related duties as required.

Authority   Performs as department head and directly supervises the work of departmental staff, including professional, paraprofessional, and clerical. Delegates specific responsibilities in a responsible manner.

Experience and Education Required

1. MLS fifth-year advanced degree with a public library Children's Services emphasis from an ALA-accredited institution is required.

2. Three (3) years successful, practical public library professional Children's Services experience required.

3. Demonstrated strong interpersonal communication skills, as well as effective oral and written presentation skills required.

4. Practical experience with electronic information delivery technology (including but not limited to online, Internet, and CD-ROM technologies) is required. Effective desktop publishing skills are desirable.

5. Demonstrated positive support/service attitude to effectively meet, communicate with, and serve the public is required.

6. Physical strength and dexterity are required to handle informational items and boxes up to 25 pounds in weight, and to transport loaded book carts; physical ability to reach items on high and low shelves is also required.

PERFORMANCE APPRAISAL

NAME (last, first):	Holly	DATE: 11/6/XX
POSITION:	Head, Children's Services	
SUPERVISOR:	Assistant Director	
BEGAN EMPLOYMENT:	9/10/XX	

The Standards of Performance system is based on the principle that an employee must know the expectations of the job and that the supervisor will inform the employee of how he or she is performing according to those expectations.

The supervisor will discuss this report with the employee and, if needed, will assist in developing an action plan for improvement.

In signing this report, the employee acknowledges having had the opportunity to review and discuss the performance appraisal, not necessarily that he or she is in agreement with the conclusions.

Upon completion and signature by employee and supervisor, this report is reviewed and signed by the Library Director.

Only the last three annual performance appraisals are kept active for review.

GUIDELINES FOR EVALUATION

- The Code of Service expresses the overall philosophy of service for Rocky River Public Library. The Code is the foundation upon which the Standards of Performance are built.

- The Standards of Performance are the types of behavior expected of an employee necessary to achieve the intent of the Code of Service.

- The Standards of Performance apply to daily performance. Throughout the year the supervisor regularly will evaluate, based on the Standards, the employee's performance.

- Effective evaluation is based on an employee's continuing pattern of behavior. Evaluation for any Standard of Performance is not based on single, unrelated actions.

- Evaluation of an employee is ongoing. When a supervisor perceives that an employee is having difficulty meeting a Standard of Performance, the supervisor is obligated to discuss with the employee what action is needed to meet the standard. The supervisor and the employee decide on the time and resources needed to meet the standard.

- For evaluation, the supervisor must document, with examples of specific, observed actions, any pattern of continuing behavior which either falls into the category of "needs improvement" (NI) or "exceeds standard" (ES). If an employee "meets standard" (MS), the supervisor has the option of either documenting or not.

- In order for an employee to receive an overall "meets standards" or "exceeds standards," the employee must have at least a 2.0 at point B2 on the tabulation sheet. This performance would reflect a level of at least "meets standards" for the employee's position responsibilities.

- Every employee's evaluation is reviewed by the Director, with the option of review by the Deputy Director.

- The employee's compensation is related directly to the employee's evaluation. The overall pattern of the evaluation determines the employee's level of compensation.

- The employee always has both the right and the responsibility to discuss with his or her immediate supervisor any disparity between the employee's interpretation of his or her behavior and the supervisor's interpretation. If the employee and the supervisor cannot come to a mutually agreeable plan of action, the Director is the final arbiter.

PERFORMANCE STANDARDS

A.	**Service to Patrons and Coworkers**	
	1. *Makes eye contact, greets others sincerely, and speaks in a friendly manner.*	ES

Comments

You maintain a consistently friendly, approachable manner, even when dealing with angry parents or upset children.

Examples of Behavior

You know your patrons very well by name or family. Whenever we discuss a patron's concerns, you frequently can offer insight into the patron's perspective. Many parents ask for you to help them because of your welcoming, friendly manner.

Action Plan

	2. *Welcomes and serves without regard to race, color, religion, gender, sexual preference, national origin, disability, age, ancestry, or other characteristics.*	ES

Comments

You initiated service to disabled children.

Examples of Behavior

You started a "special needs" collection of materials for disabled children, including descriptive videos and tactile books for the blind, and closed caption and sign language videos for the deaf. You searched for the most qualified interpreter for children's services' programming—the parents were very complimentary of this perfect match between child and interpreter. You consistently speak out at the management team meetings for enhancements to service to the disabled.

Action Plan

A.	**Service to Patrons and Coworkers** (continued)	
	3. *Acknowledges a patron's presence immediately, even if occupied.*	ES

Comments

You consistently are alert to patrons needing assistance. When you and your staff are very busy, you are able to put waiting children and parents at ease without irritating them or the people you are helping.

Examples of Behavior

Even if you are officially off-floor or are walking through the library while not on duty, you will stop to help a patron. When on duty, you consistently are sensitive to when a child needs help even though he or she has not indicated a need for assistance.

Action Plan

	4. *Does not spend an undue amount of time or effort with one patron if another patron is waiting.*	ES

Comments

Even when service demands are very high, you successfully balance the needs of those you are serving.

Examples of Behavior

I have observed on numerous occasions your calm and efficient handling of children's demands when your department is very busy (after school and around story times). You handle both in-person questions and telephone calls at the same time, juggling those with requests for computer lab sign-ups.

Action Plan

5. *Takes personal responsibility for meeting patron and staff needs correctly (informational and physical access to materials).*

ES

Comments

You are aware of and use sources in other departments to meet the needs of your patrons. You offer alternatives outside the library.

Examples of Behavior

You make a point of learning the resources of the adult services' collections (adult reference collection and the CD-ROM databases). You also work closely with the school librarians and have become familiar with the school libraries' collections. I have observed you refer parents of homeschoolers and teachers to the local university's curriculum center or to resources in area libraries.

Action Plan

6. *Does not communicate any value judgment when interacting with a patron.*

MS

Comments

Examples of Behavior

Action Plan

A.	**Service to Patrons and Coworkers** (continued)	
	7. *Verifies with the patron or coworker that his or her needs have been met.*	ES

Comments

You consistently check with the children to make sure they have found what they need.

Examples of Behavior

Through your example and the departmental training you initiated, you have set a standard and environment for verifying that your patrons are finding what they need.

Action Plan

---

	8. *Implements appropriate use of technology.*	ES

Comments

On your own, you continually update your technology skills. You are a resource person to whom staff (both adult and children's services) turn to when they have questions.

Examples of Behavior

After you researched what the schools are using and discussed options with the other departmental supervisors, you initiated a proposal for an "after-school" computer lab to help with homework assignments. You then were a guiding force in the computer design and setup of hardware and software. Through self-instruction, you have become proficient in using the Internet to meet public service needs and have shared what you have learned not only with your staff, but also with adult services' librarians.

Action Plan

9. *Exhibits proper telephone use and etiquette.*

ES

Comments

Because of your exemplary use of the telephone, you train others on the proper etiquette and manner of answering and transferring calls.

Examples of Behavior

You were instrumental in the selection and ordering of TTY equipment for the library. On your own, you learned how it operates and instructed the staff who would be using it on how to receive and send messages. You and a circulation staff member are working on ways to publicize its use.

Action Plan

---

10. *Exhibits a cooperative team spirit.*

ES

Comments

You consistently work hard to create a team environment, not only within your department, but also throughout the library.

Examples of Behavior

Many times I have observed you promote team spirit through public recognition of accomplishments that reflect staff working together on tasks. You regularly think of ways to pull together the entire staff to work on fun projects (e.g., the decoration of the library for the Friends' library open house; the library "dunking booth" at the Community Fair; using staff from each department to be the "extras" in the children services' play; bringing in items for the Summer Reading Program). You are very effective in blending different work styles in your department. Each of your staff members has responsibilities to match his or her abilities; together they make a productive, cooperative team.

Action Plan

A.	**Service to Patrons and Coworkers** (continued)	
	11. *Puts service above any personal activities or interests while on duty.*	MS

Comments

You put service to the public above any non-library-related activities.

Examples of Behavior

Action Plan

---

	12. *Is ready for duty at/during scheduled times.*	ES

Comments

You consistently adjust your work time in response to service demands.

Examples of Behavior

When your department is very busy, you stay later or cut your meal times short to help your staff meet service demands. You will cover the service desk yourself short notice when there is an emergency or unexpected illness that leaves the desk understaffed. You are often at the library at unscheduled times to oversee library/community-related events.

Action Plan

13. *Is attentive to others' complaints and, when applicable, refers the complaints to the appropriate level.*　ES

Comments

You are sensitive to how library operations affect public service, and you offer suggestions for dealing with patrons' understanding of library procedures.

Examples of Behavior

You consistently follow through with complaints and alert me or the Director of possible complaints. You are sensitive to patron concerns about the choice of materials within the children's collections and will alert me or the Director about these concerns. At management team meetings, you have contributed valuable ideas on making changes that affect patrons' use (and possible areas of concern) of the collections (circulation policies) and access to online sources (Internet Use Policy).

Action Plan

14. *Takes responsibility for learning updated internal procedures.*　ES

Comments

Other staff consistently look to you for answers on updated procedures.

Examples of Behavior

Since you make an effort to stay well informed about new library-wide procedures, staff turn to you for help (e.g., understanding the new features of the automated system, updated safety procedures, and the changes in the building's security system). You offered valuable suggestions, which were implemented, for revisions to the library's disaster plan, including evacuation procedures for the disabled.

Action Plan

A.	**Service to Patrons and Coworkers** (continued)	
	15. *Upholds library policies and established procedures.*	ES
	Comments	
	You support and present the most positive aspects of library policies and procedures in difficult situations.	
	Examples of Behavior	
	As building supervisor, you have handled difficult or emergency situations with diplomacy towards the patron and with concern for the library's responsibility to all patrons (e.g., the incident of the person who was "stalking" young females in the library; the enforcement of the User Behavior Policy). You served as a resource person in the writing of the Internet Use Policy and procedures.	
	Action Plan	
	16. *Upholds the intellectual freedom of the patron.*	ES
	Comments	
	You are very aware of intellectual freedom issues. You read the *Newsletter on Intellectual Freedom* regularly and share relevant information with the staff.	
	Examples of Behavior	
	You serve on the Cooperative Library System board's Committee on Intellectual Freedom Issues. This year you have been very active working with others on that committee on libraries' responses to parental concerns about Internet access in libraries.	
	Action Plan	

17. *Upholds all confidentiality rights of the patron.*

MS

Comments

Examples of Behavior

Action Plan

B.	**Personal Development**	
	1. *Plans own time to meet obligations and specified deadlines.*	ES
	Comments	
	Because of your excellent time management skills, you are able to pick up additional duties and accomplish them in a timely manner.	
	Examples of Behavior	
	You actively participate on several library-wide planning teams (disaster planning; liaison with the Friends' board; collection management team) and also closely work with community groups for library enhancements (e.g., PTAs, Junior Women's Board; Community Professional Women's task force). You delegate effectively so that you and your staff are not overburdened and can continually provide quality service.	
	Action Plan	
	2. *Actively listens to supervisor and accepts direction, seeking further advice from the supervisor as needed.*	MS
	Comments	
	Examples of Behavior	
	Action Plan	

3. *Accepts responsibility for own actions and obligations.*

ES

Comments

You take responsibility for your actions, taking corrective steps when needed.

Examples of Behavior

When working with community groups on raising funds for children's services' programs, you admit when an idea of yours does not generate the funds needed, yet you offer alternatives so that the program is not abandoned. You listened to my concerns about ongoing Internet training for your staff and searched for a cost-effective way to handle the training without disrupting public service; you initiated an innovative cooperative effort with a local business owner for staff Internet training.

Action Plan

4. *Adapts to change.*

ES

Comments

You actively help others comprehend the benefits of change.

Examples of Behavior

Through your example and cooperative approach, you have not only helped your staff see the value and necessity for Internet access, you have encouraged Internet access by both adult and audiovisual services' staff. Through discussions and presentations to all staff, you have illustrated the changes needed to enhance service to the disabled.

Action Plan

B.	**Personal Development** (continued)	
	5. *Uses library-provided means for continuing education or training.*	MS
	Comments	
	Examples of Behavior	
	Action Plan	
	6. *Communicates clearly and honestly.*	ES
	Comments	
	You communicate effectively in difficult or sensitive situations.	
	Examples of Behavior	
	As building supervisor, you have handled emergency situations and upset, angry patrons with skill and tact. Through actively listening and clear communication, you are able to diffuse potential staff conflicts before they become disruptive.	
	Action Plan	

7. *Demonstrates appropriate initiative within a team framework.*

ES

Comments

You consistently examine new service alternatives within your department and also suggest improvements in service library-wide.

Examples of Behavior

You researched the value of adding the computer "after-school lab" and successfully implemented the idea. You involved your staff in expanding the story time offerings to include "sleepy-time" and "babysit" programs. You solicited ideas for combining the adult and children's summer reading programs and generated excitement (and additional funding) for this combined program this year.

Action Plan

C. **Specific Job Standards**	
Items under this category relate directly to the individual's position description.	
1. Manages Children's Services department.	ES
Comments	
The high quality services your department offers and the obvious enthusiasm and energy of your staff dramatically illustrate a well-managed department.	
Examples of Behavior	
Through your connections with the school librarians and the PTAs, your department keeps current with school assignments and student interests. You encourage tours by community groups and students and coordinate curriculum support with teachers. You schedule staff to provide the maximum public service, whether for programming or information delivery. Your department's programming reflects the current needs of the community.	
Action Plan	
2. Manages collection development.	ES
Comments	
You have revitalized the juvenile collections through professional oversight and staff involvement.	
Examples of Behavior	
Under your guidance, your staff has completed a collection management plan for the juvenile collections. Through extensive evaluation, weeding, and ordering, the juvenile collections are current and relevant. Collection turnover rates this year have improved 10 percent over last year.	
Action Plan	

Items under this category relate directly to the individual's position description.

3. Coordinates programming for the juvenile public.   ES

    Comments

    Through your skillful management, your department delivers a variety of quality programming for all age groups to meet the public's demands.

    Examples of Behavior

    You continually evaluate the demand for new and different programming. You added a well-received "sleepy-time" program for parents and children which you will be expanding next year. You also determined a need for a "babysit" program and started a five-week session. You initiated the idea of a joint adult/children summer reading program and, with a team from both adult and children's services, found funding for the program and its publicity to make it highly successful.

    Action Plan

4. Performs public service functions, including information delivery and reader's advisory service.   ES

    Comments

    Your public service skills are exemplary—we receive many compliments from the parents and children who use your department.

    Examples of Behavior

    You are approachable and provide the same level of quality service to all patrons, regardless of age. You communicate your high standards for quality service to your staff and successfully train them in effective service.

    Action Plan

D.	**Supervisory Standards**	
	1. *Establishes cooperation and communication among staff.*	ES

Comments

You encourage and promote effective staff involvement in improving productivity and service.

Examples of Behavior

You involve your staff in seeking ways to simplify procedures and provide better service (e.g., registration process for story times; Summer Reading Program changes; weeding and ordering procedures). You worked closely with the acquisitions clerk to eliminate steps in the ordering process. You shared collection development ideas and sources for special needs patrons with the adult services department.

Action Plan

	2. *Makes appropriate decisions.*	ES

Comments

You make reliable decisions in difficult situations.

Examples of Behavior

You handle emergency and difficult situations calmly and in a manner that demonstrates concern for the welfare of the public and the library's responsibilities (e.g., unattended children at closing; securing the building when the building service staff are unexpectedly unavailable; dealing with an unanticipated downtime for our automated system with minimal disruption to service).

Action Plan

3. *Resolves problems fairly.* ES

Comments

If a problem arises, you analyze it to see why it happened and then you take corrective action.

Examples of Behavior

When a conflict arises between two of your staff members, you actively listen, gather all facts, and resolve the issue fairly. You and your staff then discuss ways to prevent similar incidents through a change either in procedures or in responsibility.

Action Plan

---

4. *Effectively and fairly manages the work flow of staff.* ES

Comments

You schedule and delegate so that your department is able to provide the greatest number of programs and services for the public.

Examples of Behavior

You have involved your staff in all areas of children's services—planning, programming, collection development, information delivery, and readers' advisory. You skillfully match a staff member's skills to a required task (e.g., Sue's aptitude for computers to the ongoing demands of the computer lab; Julie's focus on details to the ordering duties).

Action Plan

D.	**Supervisory Standards** (continued)	
	5. *Enforces all policies and work procedures fairly.*	ES
	Comments	
	You communicate the implications and rationale of policies and procedures, anticipating and handling successfully the concerns of staff.	
	Examples of Behavior	
	Under your guidance, your staff has thoroughly examined the implications of Internet access by children, has discussed in depth both policy and procedures, and has designed sessions for parents on Internet access for their children. These sessions have also helped staff understand the library's open access policy. You have also helped your staff understand the library's User Behavior Policy to ensure it is applied fairly.	
	Action Plan	
	6. *Effectively and fairly manages resources.*	ES
	Comments	
	You consistently use your resources to the best advantage and seek out ways to supplement them.	
	Examples of Behavior	
	Through your community involvement, you have been the driving force for the library receiving funding for the "after-school" computer lab and the joint Summer Reading Program.	
	Action Plan	

7. *Works effectively with staff to improve performance.* | MS

Comments

You continue to develop the potential of your staff.

Examples of Behavior

Action Plan

---

8. *Documents performance, then evaluates staff objectively and constructively, and in a timely manner.* | MS

Comments

Examples of Behavior

Action Plan

D. **Supervisory Standards** (continued)	
9. *Actively coordinates with other departments.*	ES

Comments

You recognize library-wide needs and willingly offer your department's resources to improve service.

Examples of Behavior

Through your participation on the library management team and your community involvement, you offer workable ideas to improve library-wide service. You have coordinated projects with other departments (e.g., the joint Summer Reading Program with adult services; the rearrangement of the juvenile collections with circulation services; determining with the outreach librarian procedures for delivery to homebound children). You demonstrated Internet access to the non-public service departments. You serve on several library-wide planning teams (e.g., disaster planning; long-range planning; policy review).

Action Plan

Comments by Supervisor

You have an excellent understanding of the broad issues and major changes affecting not only children's services, but overall public library service as well. This understanding, added to your grasp of community and school concerns, makes you a valuable member of the library's management team. You involve your staff in discussions, planning, and decisions for new services or enhancements to current services. Your integration of Internet access and an "after-school" computer lab in your department is a model for our library. Under your guidance your staff is well informed and well trained about technology and its impact on information delivery. A goal for next year is to examine the joint Summer Reading Program to see whether we should continue this combined adult/juvenile concept, modify it, expand the concept to other programming events (family-oriented), or accept the challenge of developing a cooperative program county-wide. A second goal is to develop with your staff, and recommend to the management team, an effective unattended-child policy and procedure.

Overall Action Plan

_____

Employee's signature   Date

_____

Supervisor's signature   Date

_____

Reviewer's signature   Date

Recommended for Level: _____

Comments by Employee

Employee's signature   Date

Supervisor's signature   Date

Reviewer's signature   Date

STANDARDS OF PERFORMANCE
TABULATION SHEET

ES = 3 points; MS = 2 points; NI = 1 point
Round all numbers to the nearest "tenth" at each step of the calculation
(except B2)—Examples: 2.41 = 2.4 and 2.75 = 2.8.

1. Determine the total number of applicable standards for each:

    Service: _17_
    Personal Development: _7_

    Total above two categories: _24_ (A)

    Specific Job Standards: _4_
    Supervisory: _9_

    Total above two categories: _13_ (B)

2. Determine point value for each of the applicable sections:

    Service:
    number of ES X 3 =_42_ number of MS X 2 =_6_ number of NI =_0_
    Total for Service Standards: _48_

    Personal Development:
    number of ES X 3 =_15_ number of MS X 2 =_4_ number of NI =_0_
    Total for Personal Development: _19_

    Grand total of above two categories: _67_ (A1)

    Specific Job Standards:
    number of ES X 3 =_12_ number of MS X 2 =_0_ number of NI =_0_
    Total for Specific Job Standards: _12_

    Supervisory:
    number of ES X 3 =_21_ number of MS X 2 =_4_ number of NI =_0_
    Total for Supervisory Standards: _25_

    Grand total of above two categories: _37_ (B1)

3. To determine the overall point value for Service and Development sections:

    Take **A1** _67_ and divide by **A** _24_

    This results in **A2:** _2.8_ (the value for these sections)

4. To determine overall point value for the specific Job Standards and Supervisors:

    Take **B1** _37_ and divide by **B** _13_

    This results in **B2:** _2.8_ * (the value for these sections)

    > *** B2:**
    > **Must be 2.0 or higher to proceed with calculation.**

5. To determine overall point value for this evaluation:

    Add **A2** _2.8_ to **B2** _2.8_ This results in **B3:** _5.6_

    Now divide **B3** by 2 _2.8_ This is the total point value for this evaluation

    Using this number, the **overall evaluation** is rated _ES_

ES	= 2.5 or higher
MS3	= 2.4–2.2
MS2	= 2.1–1.8
MS1	= 1.7–1.5
NI	= 1.4 or lower

Employee's name: _____

Supervisor's signature: _____

Date: _____

Problem Employee

Betty
Assistant Supervisor, Adult Services

Since each standard in this performance appraisal system has guidelines indicating the various levels of behavior (meets, exceeds, or needs improvement), both supervisor and employee know precisely what types of behavior will elicit what rating. A supervisor who sees a pattern of "needs improvement" behavior always documents examples of that behavior. Coaching then takes place to try to bring that employee to a "meets standard" level.

Sometimes—no matter how much coaching an employee receives—the employee makes no effort to change the unacceptable behaviors, and the supervisor must rate the employee as an overall "needs improvement." If the supervisor is evaluating a staff member who also supervises, the difficulty of the situation increases.

Expected Behaviors for Quality Service

Using the objective, library-wide guidelines attached to each standard (see the Standards of Performance Guidelines, Appendix B), the supervisor can offer specific examples of behavior without becoming personal or criticizing attitudes. Remember that attitudes are very difficult to alter, if at all, as opposed to behaviors which an employee, if motivated, can adjust. Behaviors cause reactions from others and can be evaluated by someone else. If I snarl at you, you probably will stomp away in anger and perhaps complain to someone. If I smile and welcome you in a friendly manner, you probably will carry on a pleasant conversation with me. A supervisor can coach an employee on the expected behaviors for quality service.

Documenting "Needs Improvement" Behaviors

For a "needs improvement" rating, it is important to document examples (with dates, if feasible); discuss the examples with the employee as close to the date of occurrence as possible (or, if there are several standards for which there are unacceptable behaviors, schedule a review meeting); and set achievable action plans for improvement. If the employee does not cooperate with the coaching process and shows little or no progress in changing behaviors, the supervisor has the written documentation already in place for whatever action is determined to be appropriate.

The termination procedure is specific to the individual library. One library may state that an overall "needs improvement" evaluation results in dismissal. Another library may state that the employee must have two consecutive "needs improvement" evaluations (whether overall or in section C, Specific Job Standards, of the Performance Appraisal document, Appendix D). Whatever your library determines is the criterion for dismissal, it should be a part of the library's personnel policies to ensure it is consistent library-wide.

A Need to Change Behaviors

In the case that follows, Betty, a long-term employee, became assistant supervisor of adult services almost by default. Now, under a new administration with a focus on proactive public service, Betty is faced with changing her behaviors to meet the expectations of quality service. Her new supervisor uses the performance document as a tool to coach Betty. When the coaching does not produce the desired adjustments in behaviors, Betty's supervisor is prepared for the final "needs improvement" evaluation and review.

Betty

Background

Betty, who received her MLS thirty years ago, is currently the assistant supervisor under the head of adult services. Betty, who worked for the library for ten years as a reference librarian, was made assistant supervisor three years ago. The previous director of the library was worried about the health of the head of adult services and appointed Betty as assistant supervisor (a newly created position) just in case the head of the department was absent on a long sick leave. The director did not post or advertise the position and chose Betty because she had seniority. The head of adult services had no say in the matter. Betty was made responsible for reference service, including acquisition for and maintenance of the adult reference collection and recommendations to the head of adult services on enhancements or changes to the delivery of reference services to the public. Her duties also included supervising the library shelving staff (five high school students and two adults) and assuming the duties of the head of adult services in her absence.

Shortly after Betty's advancement to the position of assistant supervisor, the head of adult services had a serious operation. Betty was made acting head of adult services for three months. Betty basically was a "caretaker" for the department and its services; she made no changes even though there were numerous complaints of uneven and poor service. One year later, the library's director moved out-of-state to take another job, and the still-ailing head of adult services announced her intent to retire.

A New Director Brings Change

The new director was hired with a mandate from the library's board of trustees (among other recommended administrative and policy changes) to emphasize the most modern methods of reference service, including the latest technology. One of the new director's first acts was to hire a replacement for the retiring head of adult services. The job was posted internally, as well as outside the library, and Betty did apply. Betty indicated to several staff members that the new director "would be a fool not to take advantage of my experience and obvious outstanding knowledge of the collection." After all, she said, she had "proven her loyalty" by taking on the duties of the head of adult services with little complaint for three months. However, the new director surprised the staff—and especially Betty—by hiring a recent MLS graduate with two years' professional experience in the reference department of a busy metropolitan library and an undergraduate degree in business management.

Outlining Expectations for Service

The new head of adult services, Linda, accepted the position with the understanding that the director wanted dramatic changes in the adult services department. One of the first steps Linda took was to examine the print reference collection. She found it to be in excellent shape—current and relevant to the needs of the community. Linda also immediately interviewed her staff.

When she met with Betty, Linda complimented her on the quality of the reference collection. Betty's response was that she "had spent years building the collection and did not want to see it destroyed by spending money on technological fads that no one would use or understand." Linda conveyed the seriousness of the directive from the director and the trustees and her interest in looking at alternative reference sources such as CD-ROM databases and Internet access. Betty's response was that she thought the new director was causing too much disruption for no good reason. In addition, Betty said, the new director wanted all staff to wear name badges and greet all patrons who came into the building. "Well," said Betty, "I've worked here for more than ten years and I will greet whomever I want—there are some patrons I wouldn't give the time of day to, so I certainly won't say hello to them!" Betty went on to lecture Linda on how things had always been done at this library and how it was all fine before this new director took over. "Just follow me, my dear," Betty said, "and I'll show you how we do things around here."

Observation of Behaviors

Linda did watch Betty carefully over the next several weeks. Linda had to admit that Betty knew what she was doing when it came to answering reference questions. She knew the sources in-depth and answered questions quickly and accurately. However, Linda noticed other things as well. Betty had obvious favorites. She would spend much time with older patrons or members of the women's clubs of which Betty was also a member. She spent very little time or was abrupt with mothers with young children. "Don't these mothers know that the library is not a place for screaming kids?" was a comment Linda overheard her make many times. Betty totally ignored any school-aged students. Linda noticed that the other reference librarians (who had worked under Betty when she was head of adult services) were afraid to say anything to Betty. Some staff members (not from the reference department) and two other supervisors did mention to Linda that Betty was making disparaging remarks about several of the new policies.

Examples of Behaviors

At departmental meetings, Betty invariably would stop a discussion with an explanation of how "we tried that a couple of years ago and it didn't work" or would state the difficulties of what Linda was proposing. Often what Betty had to say was relevant; she did have good points, but was so adamant in her opinions that she did not hear what other staff were trying to express. Consequently, the meetings were not as productive as Linda would have liked. Linda encouraged all staff to participate in discussions, but several of the departmental members would fall silent when Betty forcefully voiced her opinions.

The name badges were an obvious irritant to Betty. Because Linda knew the name badges were unpopular with many of her staff, she tried to be as kind as possible about reminding staff. Betty would listen to Linda with a grim mouth and when Linda was working with her, Betty did wear the name badge. Other times, Linda noticed that Betty would put the name badge on a sweater or jacket which she then would throw over a chair. When Linda reminded Betty that the name badge had to be visible to the public, Betty would exclaim, "Oh, how silly of me! I had gotten warm running around helping all these people while you were off meeting with the director, and I just forgot the name badge was on the jacket I had taken off."

Linda was quickly moving ahead with adding CD-ROM-based resources and was putting together a task force to implement Internet access. Linda started an in-house training program for her staff and scheduled each of them off-floor to work on learning the skills needed to access the electronic resources. Betty continued to resist. She reluctantly used the automated catalog ("It was a sad day when the card catalog disappeared," was her mantra). She had never bothered to learn the advanced searching techniques on the automated catalog, relying instead on her knowledge of several print sources for the questions she chose to answer.

Linda soon noticed that the student shelvers would avoid asking Betty for help with their duties. Instead, they would turn to other members of the reference staff for help. Consequently, the shelving would back up unless one of the adult shelvers said something to Betty who would then rearrange the scheduling of duties.

Setting Action Plans

Throughout the year, Linda held several private meetings with Betty and set up specific action plans. Betty was to wear her name badge so that it was always visible to the public. She was to learn how to search in one CD-ROM resource per quarter. She was to attend refresher training on the automated system and apply the advanced searching techniques. She was designated to take at least one reference question from a school-aged child each day. Linda reviewed with Betty the steps in meeting with the shelvers for their evaluations. Linda also outlined what her expectations, as head of adult services, were for the growth of the reference collections, the addition of electronic services, and the importance of Betty's assistance in evaluating electronic resources and training staff in their use.

Linda carefully documented her meetings with Betty, noting and reviewing with her examples of observable behaviors. She also documented the action plans and the results. Linda also fairly applied the library's progressive discipline procedures. When it was time for Betty's end-of-year appraisal, Linda was prepared.

JOB DESCRIPTION
ASSISTANT SUPERVISOR, ADULT SERVICES

Position Title   Assistant Supervisor, Adult Services

Reports to   Head, Adult Services

Category   Professional

Grade   Level 1 or above

Classification   Full-time, exempt

Responsibility   To implement effective Adult Reference Collection management, to practice responsive personnel procedures (including hiring, evaluation, and supervision) with the Reference Department's shelving staff, and to support the direct provision of information service to adult and young adult users while demonstrating courtesy, resourcefulness, and sound judgment.

Duties

*1. Maintain relevancy of Adult Reference Collection by approving titles for acquisition, renewal, or removal either directly—or with supervisor's approval—through assignment to departmental members.

*2. Identify and recommend Adult Reference service changes including the application of Adult Reference information technology.

*3. Supervise and schedule Adult Reference shelving staff; recommend appropriate personnel actions including hiring, promotion, demotion, separation, performance evaluation, and performance coaching.

*4. Provide instruction in Reference Services delivery methods and technical training for all members of the Adult Reference staff.

*5. Provide direct (floor) service to support both adult and young adult general reference activity.

*6. Participate in adult circulation book selection utilizing approved professional techniques and sources; support currency and quality of existing adult circulating nonfiction collection through periodic holdings review and timely weeding.

7. Coordinate annual inventory of Adult Reference Collection.

*Indicates essential functions of this position.

8. Attend professional meetings designed to encourage the delivery of effective adult reference and young adult information services.

9. Perform other related duties as required.

Authority   Performs as a staff supervisor and directly oversees the work of the Adult Reference shelving staff while under the authority of Head, Adult Services. Performs assigned duties of Head, Adult Services in his/her absence.

Experience and Education Required

1. MLS fifth-year advanced degree from an ALA-accredited institution required.

2. Two years successful, practical public library Adult Reference experience in a positive service environment required.

3. Demonstrated strong adult and young adult level interpersonal communication skills required.

4. Practical experience with electronic information delivery technology, as well as effective computer skills, required.

5. Physical strength and dexterity are required to handle informational items and boxes up to 25 pounds in weight, and to transport loaded book carts; physical ability to reach items on high and low shelves is also required.

PERFORMANCE APPRAISAL

NAME (last, first):   Betty   DATE: 11/4/XX

POSITION: Assistant Supervisor, Adult Services

SUPERVISOR: Head, Adult Services

BEGAN EMPLOYMENT: 10/12/XX

The Standards of Performance system is based on the principle that an employee must know the expectations of the job and that the supervisor will inform the employee of how he or she is performing according to those expectations.

The supervisor will discuss this report with the employee and, if needed, will assist in developing an action plan for improvement.

In signing this report, the employee acknowledges having had the opportunity to review and discuss the performance appraisal, not necessarily that he or she is in agreement with the conclusions.

Upon completion and signature by employee and supervisor, this report is reviewed and signed by the Library Director.

Only the last three annual performance appraisals are kept active for review.

GUIDELINES FOR EVALUATION

- The Code of Service expresses the overall philosophy of service for Rocky River Public Library. The Code is the foundation upon which the Standards of Performance are built.

- The Standards of Performance are the types of behavior expected of an employee necessary to achieve the intent of the Code of Service.

- The Standards of Performance apply to daily performance. Throughout the year the supervisor regularly will evaluate, based on the Standards, the employee's performance.

- Effective evaluation is based on an employee's continuing pattern of behavior. Evaluation for any Standard of Performance is not based on single, unrelated actions.

- Evaluation of an employee is ongoing. When a supervisor perceives that an employee is having difficulty meeting a Standard of Performance, the supervisor is obligated to discuss with the employee what action is needed to meet the standard. The supervisor and the employee decide on the time and resources needed to meet the standard.

- For evaluation, the supervisor must document, with examples of specific, observed actions, any pattern of continuing behavior which either falls into the category of "needs improvement" (NI) or "exceeds standard" (ES). If an employee "meets standard" (MS), the supervisor has the option of either documenting or not.

- In order for an employee to receive an overall "meets standards" or "exceeds standards," the employee must have at least a 2.0 at point B2 on the tabulation sheet. This performance would reflect a level of at least "meets standards" for the employee's position responsibilities.

- Every employee's evaluation is reviewed by the Director, with the option of review by the Deputy Director.

- The employee's compensation is related directly to the employee's evaluation. The overall pattern of the evaluation determines the employee's level of compensation.

- The employee always has both the right and the responsibility to discuss with his or her immediate supervisor any disparity between the employee's interpretation of his or her behavior and the supervisor's interpretation. If the employee and the supervisor cannot come to a mutually agreeable plan of action, the Director is the final arbiter.

PERFORMANCE STANDARDS

A. **Service to Patrons and Coworkers**	

1. *Makes eye contact, greets others sincerely, and speaks in a friendly manner.* **NI**

Comments

You are pleasant only to people you like or know.

Examples of Behavior

On several occasions I have spoken to you about your abrupt manner with patrons: 2/5; 3/11; 3/22; 4/13. We met on 5/1 to discuss the comments from staff and patrons about your unwelcoming behaviors. Since that meeting, the mid-year review on 7/8, and the subsequent meeting on 8/26, you continue to be unpleasant and curt with people whom you dislike.

Action Plan

Be welcoming and pleasant to every patron you meet. Once a week for a three-hour period, serve the public from service desk #1, which receives the most walk-in patrons. Look up with a smile when a patron approaches you.

---

2. *Welcomes and serves without regard to race, color, religion, gender, sexual preference, national origin, disability, age, ancestry, or other characteristics.* **NI**

Comments

You do not give the same quality of service to everyone.

Examples of Behavior

You avoid helping school-aged children. The action plan we agreed upon on 5/1 requires you to assist at least one school-aged child each day you work at the service desk. You have not fulfilled that requirement consistently.

Action Plan

Consistently and completely help one school-aged child with a reference question every day you work at the service desk.

3. *Acknowledges a patron's presence immediately, even if occupied.*   NI

Comments

You are so preoccupied with other patrons with whom you are chatting, you do not notice other patrons who need assistance.

Examples of Behavior

On many occasions I have observed you ignoring other patrons while you were conversing with patrons (2/3; 3/8; 3/9; 4/2; 4/5). We met on 5/1 and discussed this issue.

Action Plan

Acknowledge waiting patrons with a smile or comment.

4. *Does not spend an undue amount of time or effort with one patron if another patron is waiting.*   NI

Comments

You "choose" which patrons you will assist with a reference question and will not help another patron who is waiting.

Examples of Behavior

On numerous occasions I have observed you "hand over" a patron to another librarian without making the effort of getting the patron started with possible sources. At both your mid-year review and the follow-up meeting on 8/26, I emphasized the importance of taking reference questions as they come, and not picking the ones with which you are most comfortable answering. You continue to "pick and choose" the reference questions you will assist with, resulting in uneven service to waiting patrons.

Action Plan

For the next six weeks, I am scheduling you to work with me or another designated librarian. During that time, you are to help patrons in the order they approach the service desk.

A.	**Service to Patrons and Coworkers** (continued)	

5. *Takes personal responsibility for meeting patron and staff needs correctly (informational and physical access to materials).*   **MS**

Comments

Examples of Behavior

Action Plan

6. *Does not communicate any value judgment when interacting with a patron.*   **NI**

Comments

On several occasions I have observed you commenting negatively to patrons (and also to staff in situations where you could be easily overheard by patrons) about the patron's reference or reading requests.

Examples of Behavior

These comments ranged from criticisms about the type of questions school-aged children were asking (5/16; 6/3; 7/12) to derogatory remarks about requested fiction titles (5/26; 6/10; 8/6). I have spoken to you about not making such remarks (see notes from meetings of 5/1 and 8/26 and your mid-year appraisal), yet you have persisted in doing so.

Action Plan

Do not offer unsolicited negative comments to patrons or to other staff about patrons' requests.

7. *Verifies with the patron or coworker that his or her needs have been met.* | NI

Comments

You do not consistently check with patrons to see if they are finding what they need.

Examples of Behavior

You frequently leave patrons in the stacks on their own. You only check back with patrons whom you know personally or through your volunteer work. Again, the need to follow through with patrons, checking that they are finding what they need, was a point discussed at our action plan meetings of 5/1 and 8/26 and at your mid-year appraisal review. However, you have not changed your behavior.

Action Plan

After assisting patrons, consistently verify that their needs have been met by checking with them before they leave the building.

8. *Implements appropriate use of technology.* | NI

Comments

You refuse to learn technology useful for your duties.

Examples of Behavior

As assistant supervisor of adult services, your responsibilities include the identification and recommendation of technology for adult reference. I indicated to you at the 5/1 meeting that I expected you to review and recommend at least two electronic reference resources by September 1. You have not done so. Your reference duties include searching the automated catalog. You have not applied the advanced searching techniques you have learned at the refresher training that we set up for you after your action plan meetings and mid-year review.

Action Plan

Knowing and using advanced searching techniques on the automated catalog is vital to your duties. Review the "how to search" brochure and ask the system administrator for assistance if needed. Within six weeks, demonstrate to me what you have learned.

A.	**Service to Patrons and Coworkers** (continued)	
	9. *Exhibits proper telephone use and etiquette.*	MS
	Comments	
	Examples of Behavior	
	Action Plan	
	10. *Exhibits a cooperative team spirit.*	NI
	Comments	
	You use intimidating behaviors to get your way with your coworkers.	
	Examples of Behavior	
	At our departmental meetings you frequently make disparaging remarks about the opinions of other staff. On several occasions I have observed you refuse to change your actions to accommodate the needs of your coworkers. It was only through my intervention that the situations were defused. (For example, refusing to cooperate during the massive inventory project; not placing orders for reference titles suggested by other reference librarians; neglecting to take your turn with the more mundane tasks at the service desk such as checking requests for titles not owned).	
	Action Plan	
	Offer your help to your coworkers whenever possible.	

11. *Puts service above any personal activities or interests while on duty.*

MS

Comments

Examples of Behavior

Action Plan

12. *Is ready for duty at/during scheduled times.*

MS

Comments

Examples of Behavior

Action Plan

A. **Service to Patrons and Coworkers** (continued)	

13. *Is attentive to others' complaints and, when applicable, refers the complaints to the appropriate level.* — NI

Comments

You do not inform me of complaints from patrons or other staff.

Examples of Behavior

On three occasions, patrons have come to me asking why we did not add specific titles they requested for the collection after they had asked you about those titles. Since you had not informed me of their complaints, I had to research their requests before answering them accurately—an unacceptable delay in our policy of answering patrons' complaints within 48 hours. You "brush off" the complaints of those with whom you disagree and do not follow through with referring their concerns to me or to the director.

Action Plan

Refer <u>all</u> complaints to me, regardless of your opinion of their validity.

14. *Takes responsibility for learning updated internal procedures.* — MS

Comments

You attend meetings regularly and are aware of departmental procedural changes.

Examples of Behavior

Action Plan

15. *Upholds library policies and established procedures.* NI

Comments

You consistently and in front of patrons openly criticize and ignore library policies that you personally do not like.

Examples of Behavior

Many times I have reminded you about the library's policy for wearing a name badge, yet you frequently do not wear your name badge. You do not enforce the library's User Behavior Policy. Three times you permitted a reference volume to leave the building, even though it is against policy.

Action Plan

Review these policies: User Behavior, Collection Management, and the Personnel Code on Employee Conduct (section 8). Do not deviate from the policies without my approval.

---

16. *Upholds the intellectual freedom of the patron.* MS

Comments

Examples of Behavior

Action Plan

A.	**Service to Patrons and Coworkers** (continued)	
	17. *Upholds all confidentiality rights of the patron.*	MS
	Comments	
	Examples of Behavior	
	Action Plan	

B. **Personal Development**	
1. *Plans own time to meet obligations and specified deadlines.*	MS

Comments

Examples of Behavior

Action Plan

2. *Actively listens to supervisor and accepts direction, seeking further advice from the supervisor as needed.*	NI

Comments

You do not accept direction from me, your supervisor.

Examples of Behavior

For all the "needs improvements" in this document, throughout the year I have suggested action plans for improvement to a "meets standard" level. You have not accepted my direction or sought my advice for alternative ways for you to provide the quality service expected.

Action Plan

Do not deviate from my directions. If you do not understand or you disagree, check with me about alternatives.

B.	**Personal Development** (continued)	
	3. *Accepts responsibility for own actions and obligations.*	NI

Comments

You neither admit when you are wrong nor accept constructive criticism.

Examples of Behavior

Even though you and I have met throughout the year to discuss the types of behaviors to support quality service, you have not followed the action plans we set up to correct unacceptable behaviors (see standards with "needs improvement"). You insist on behaviors that do not provide quality service.

Action Plan

Actively listen to my suggestions for improvement and accept the action plans.

	4. *Adapts to change.*	NI

Comments

You refuse to adhere to new policies and actively campaign against them.

Examples of Behavior

Through your comments and actions you attempt to undermine new policies and procedures. Examples: belittling in front of other staff and patrons the wearing of name badges; criticizing to patrons and any staff who will listen the library's focus on adding new electronic resources; ignoring the new procedures I set up in the department.

Action Plan

Do not criticize in front of patrons or other staff any library policy or procedure.

5. *Uses library-provided means for continuing education or training.*	MS

Comments

You attend required meetings and training.

Examples of Behavior

Action Plan

6. *Communicates clearly and honestly.*	NI

Comments

You frequently are deliberately deceptive.

Examples of Behavior

During and after our several private meetings throughout the year, I have checked with you on the status of changing your behaviors. You frequently indicated to me that you were "working on" changing the unacceptable behaviors. Later, through your actions and comments from other supervisors, I learned that while you were agreeing with me to my face, at the same time, you would be saying the exact opposite to other staff.

Action Plan

Tell me directly when you disagree with me; do not voice your disagreements with me or the director behind our backs.

B. Personal Development (continued)

7. *Demonstrates appropriate initiative within a team framework.* NI

   ### Comments

   You act independently of the department and your coworkers.

   ### Examples of Behavior

   You do not assist your coworkers when needed. You do not discuss with your coworkers or with me changes in the standing orders for reference titles. You discard titles from the reference collection without informing me or your coworkers.

   ### Action Plan

   Discuss with me or at a departmental meeting any changes to the reference collection—before you implement them.

C.	**Specific Job Standards**	
	Items under this category relate directly to the individual's position description.	
	1. Maintain relevancy of the adult reference collection through timely acquisitions, weeding, and review.	MS
	Comments	
	The print adult reference collection is current.	
	Examples of Behavior	
	Action Plan	
	2. Identify and recommend adult reference service changes including the application of information technology; provide appropriate training.	NI
	Comments	
	You have not recommended service changes and have not provided appropriate training.	
	Examples of Behavior	
	See standard A8. See minutes of our meetings of 5/1, 7/8, and 8/26.	
	Action Plan	
	See Supervisor's comments at end of document.	

C.	**Specific Job Standards** (continued)	
	Items under this category relate directly to the individual's position description.	
	3. Supervise and schedule adult reference shelving staff; recommend appropriate personnel actions.	NI
	Comments	
	You do not effectively provide appropriate supervision of the adult services shelving staff.	
	Examples of Behavior	
	You are not aware of work flow problems until other reference librarians point them out. You do not regularly meet with the staff under your direct supervision. Due to inadequate training and supervision there has been a high turnover of student shelving staff.	
	Action Plan	
	See Supervisor's comments at end of document.	
	4. Provide direct (floor) service to support both adult and young adult general reference activity.	NI
	Comments	
	You provide uneven service.	
	Examples of Behavior	
	See standards A1, A2, A4, A6, A7.	
	Action Plan	
	See Supervisor's comments at end of document.	

Items under this category relate directly to the individual's position description.

5. Participate in adult circulation book selection utilizing approved professional techniques and sources.　　　MS

　　　Comments

　　　Examples of Behavior

　　　Action Plan

D.	Supervisory Standards	
	1. *Establishes cooperation and communication among staff.*	NI

Comments

You do not listen to concerns of your staff. There is a very obvious division between the student and adult shelvers.

Examples of Behavior

There is no team spirit in the staff you supervise. The student shelvers have commented to me that they feel neglected and sometimes do not know what they are supposed to be doing when they finish their shelving sections. You do not schedule shelving staff meetings. You do not communicate through e-mail with your staff.

Action Plan

See Supervisor's comments at end of document.

	2. *Makes appropriate decisions.*	NI

Comments

You either make a decision with insufficient information or you do not make a decision at all.

Examples of Behavior

You have contributed to poor service situations by not making decisions when necessary. (For example, as building supervisor, you did not make decisions about work flow issues in the circulation department when the circulation supervisor was not available; consequently, there were too few staff at the checkout counter at busy times. You indiscriminately "evict" students after school without knowing whether they are the ones causing trouble).

Action Plan

See Supervisor's comments at end of document.

3. *Resolves problems fairly.* **NI**

Comments

You complain about problems frequently, but do not take steps to resolve them.

Examples of Behavior

You complain to other staff about the "mess" the return/sorting room is, but you do not work with the head of circulation services or with your shelving staff to rearrange the shelves or to discuss the procedures for handling returned library materials. You complain about students using adult reference titles in the children's area, but do not check with the children's services librarians to see if duplicate titles could be ordered or if some titles should be switched to the children's reference collection.

Action Plan

See Supervisor's comments at end of document.

4. *Effectively and fairly manages the work flow of staff.* **NI**

Comments

You do not effectively and fairly manage the work flow of the shelving staff under your supervision.

Examples of Behavior

The shelving and shelf reading are consistently backlogged. Both the heads of circulation services and technical services have frequently complained to me about misshelved items or unshelved items sitting in the sorting room for days. You do not schedule your staff fairly. Adult shelvers are often working on nonshelving projects when the shelving is backed up.

Action Plan

See Supervisor's comments at end of document.

D.	**Supervisory Standards** (continued)	
	5. *Enforces all policies and work procedures fairly.*	NI
	Comments	
	You favor the adult shelvers over the student shelvers.	
	Examples of Behavior	
	You change the student shelvers' schedules abruptly. You do not offer them the same variety of projects you offer the adult shelvers. Acting in my place while I was on vacation, you permitted one librarian to adjust her schedule to accommodate a personal need, yet refused another librarian with a similar request.	
	Action Plan	
	See Supervisor's comments at end of document.	
	6. *Effectively and fairly manages resources.*	NI
	Comments	
	You frequently do not plan the activities of the shelving staff under your supervision.	
	Examples of Behavior	
	There is a consistent backlog of items waiting to be shelved, which prevents having items available for use (poor service). You do not effectively schedule your staff to handle peak periods of returned items.	
	Action Plan	
	See Supervisor's comments at end of document.	

7. *Works effectively with staff to improve performance.*   NI

   Comments

   You seldom meet with your staff and do not work with them to improve performance.

   Examples of Behavior

   Performance levels for your staff are uneven, resulting in poor service to both staff and the public. I have received complaints from supervisors of other departments (circulation, adult, and children's) and have conveyed those complaints to you for action. You have not addressed any of the performance issues.

   Action Plan

   See Supervisor's comments at end of document.

8. *Documents performance, then evaluates staff objectively and constructively, and in a timely manner.*   NI

   Comments

   You do not follow the Supervisory Procedures for Conducting a Performance Evaluation.

   Examples of Behavior

   You do not hold the scheduled performance review meetings with your staff. You document very few "examples of behavior" for "needs improvement" or "exceeds standard."

   Action Plan

   See Supervisor's comments at end of document.

9. *Actively coordinates with other departments.*   NI

Comments

You do not cooperate with other departments.

Examples of Behavior

You refused to cooperate with children's services when they needed extra shelving help after a hectic day of story times and programming. You delayed the security stripping of the reference titles by not coordinating work schedules with technical services. You first agreed to "loan" some of your shelvers for the in-house survey, but then, at the last minute, reneged on the agreement.

Action Plan

See Supervisor's comments at end of document.

Comments by Supervisor

Because you are "needs improvement" for your job duties (section C, Specific Job Standards, and section D, Supervisory Standards), I am recommending to the director that you be relieved of your supervisory duties. According to the library's Personnel Code, if an employee has had six months or more of coaching and review meetings to improve performance, and still has an end-of-appraisal year rating of "needs improvement" in his or her job duties, the supervisor can recommend to the director that the employee be demoted or discharged. Based on your continual and willful refusal this past appraisal year to change your unacceptable behaviors as noted in this document, I am recommending to the director your demotion. I am also recommending that if you do not improve at least 80 percent of your "needs improvement" standards in sections A, B, and C of this document to "meets standard" within the next six weeks, you be discharged.

Overall Action Plan

To continue as a reference librarian of our library, follow the action plans in sections A and B and improve your performance to a "meets standards" level for 80 percent of your "needs improvement" standards. This improvement must be evident within the next six-week period. During this time frame, I will schedule you at the service desk with myself or another designated librarian who will give you immediate feedback on your actions. After the previous six months of continual coaching, this six-week period is your final opportunity to demonstrate your willingness to adjust your behaviors to meet the standard of quality service this library provides. If you do not demonstrate this acceptable level of improvement in your behaviors, you will be discharged. You do have the option of appealing my decision to the director. (See section 10.2 of the Personnel Code for the procedure.)

Employee's signature   Date

Supervisor's signature   Date

Reviewer's signature   Date

Recommended for Level: _____

Comments by Employee

This place has become too picky for me. No one ever worried about what I was doing before, and I think I was doing fine. I don't see the purpose of changing now. If you don't appreciate me, I'll be glad to get out of this place. You can consider this my "formal" resignation.

_____

Employee's signature   Date

_____

Supervisor's signature   Date

_____

Reviewer's signature   Date

STANDARDS OF PERFORMANCE
TABULATION SHEET

ES = 3 points; MS = 2 points; NI = 1 point
Round all numbers to the nearest "tenth" at each step of the calculation
(except B2)—Examples: 2.41 = 2.4 and 2.75 = 2.8.

1. Determine the total number of applicable standards for each:

    Service: _17_
    Personal Development: _7_

    Total above two categories: _24_ (A)

    Specific Job Standards: _5_
    Supervisory: _9_

    Total above two categories: _14_ (B)

2. Determine point value for each of the applicable sections:

    Service:
    number of ES X 3 = _0_ number of MS X 2 = _14_ number of NI = _10_
    Total for Service Standards: _24_

    Personal Development:
    number of ES X 3 = _0_ number of MS X 2 = _4_ number of NI = _5_
    Total for Personal Development: _9_

    Grand total of above two categories: _33_ (A1)

    Specific Job Standards:
    number of ES X 3 = _0_ number of MS X 2 = _4_ number of NI = _3_
    Total for Specific Job Standards: _7_

    Supervisory:
    number of ES X 3 = _0_ number of MS X 2 = _0_ number of NI = _9_
    Total for Supervisory Standards: _9_

    Grand total of above two categories: _16_ (B1)

STANDARDS OF PERFORMANCE
TABULATION SHEET

3. To determine the overall point value for Service and Development sections:

   Take **A1** _33_ and divide by **A** _24_

   This results in **A2**: _1.4_ (the value for these sections)

4. To determine overall point value for the specific Job Standards and Supervisors:

   Take **B1** _16_ and divide by **B** _14_

   This results in **B2**: _1.1_ * (the value for these sections)

   ---
   * B2:
   Must be 2.0 or higher to proceed with calculation.
   ---

5. To determine overall point value for this evaluation:

   Add **A2** _____ to **B2** _____ This results in **B3**: _____

   Now divide **B3** by 2 _____ This is the total point value for this evaluation

   Using this number, the **overall evaluation** is rated _____

ES	= 2.5 or higher
MS3	= 2.4–2.2
MS2	= 2.1–1.8
MS1	= 1.7–1.5
NI	= 1.4 or lower

Employee's name: _____

Supervisor's signature:_____

Date: _____

Non-Public Service Employee

Gary
Technical Services Assistant

T his performance appraisal system, with its focus on behaviors and actions that support a service ethic, is practical for employees who have no direct contact or who do not interact with a library's public (whether patrons, clients, students, faculty, or business people). Even if an employee is in a non-public service position, his or her actions significantly contribute to the overall service the library provides; this performance appraisal system reflects that correlation.

Non-Public Service Employees

For example, if a maintenance employee does not keep the building environment safe, healthy, and functional (i.e., the lights work, the temperature is bearable, equipment is operable, and furniture is usable), the employees of the library are not able to provide optimal service to the public or the library's clients. If a technical services employee does not process received library materials in a timely and efficient manner, neither the public service staff nor the library's users have access to needed items. If the library's finance or business staff does not pay invoices on time or does not issue accurate fund information, staff buying the library's materials are not able to purchase needed materials and, again, overall service suffers.

The connection between a non-public service employee and the public or clients the library serves is usually through another employee. Section A of the Performance Appraisal document (Appendix D) is worded as "Service to Patrons and Coworkers" to emphasize that connection. If a non-public service employee meets or exceeds the standards in section A, overall service is enhanced and the values set forth in the library's Code of Service are reinforced daily.

"Not Applicable" Standards

Of all the employees in a library setting, it is most likely that the supervisor of a non-public service department or staff will note NA or "not applicable" for some standards in Section A. Examples include standards A16 and A17 (Appendix D). It is an unusual library (but still a possibility) that presents opportunities for its building services or technical services staff to "uphold the intellectual freedom of the patron" (standard A16). If opportunities for staff of a particular department to meet or exceed a specific standard do not exist, it is not fair to evaluate those employees on that individual standard. On the other hand, it is not wise to assume automatically that such opportunities are not available to non-public service employees. For example, staff of a library's business or finance office may have multiple occasions to view or handle confidential information connecting patrons to items they borrow (e.g., payments for lost or damaged library materials, collection of fees for long overdue materials) and have the ability to meet, exceed, or need improvement for standard A17 ("upholds all confidentiality rights of the patron").

Depending upon a library's policies or procedures for staff development or growth, non-public as well as public service staff may have the same opportunities to meet all the standards. A library could require all staff to attend intellectual freedom training sessions. A non-public service employee could exceed standard A16 by going beyond the library-mandated requirements, reading more about the issue, and then enlightening other staff members about intellectual freedom issues relevant to the library's service.

Be Consistent

What is most vital to remember in assigning NA or "not applicable" to standards is consistency. A supervisor definitely must be consistent—all employees in the same category or classification within the department should have the same number of standards which are applicable to that specific job category or classification. In short, two employees doing the same job should not be evaluated on a different number of standards.

Gary

The Hiring

After working part-time as a library shelving clerk for financial aid in college, Gary expressed an interest in library work as a career. He had originally thought he would study to become a lawyer, but soon decided he did not want that kind of pressure for better grades. A political science major with an average grade cumulative, he decided that he could no longer work and go to school at the same time. Instead, he chose to work for a few years and save enough money to return to school full-time.

He thought he would prefer the "order and steadiness" of technical services work. He had indicated in his interview that he "liked detail work" and "didn't mind repetitive tasks at all." As a shelver, he had enjoyed putting the library's books and bound periodicals in order and had been commended for shelving accurately and for keeping the shelves neat and organized. He had his own personal computer at home and often spent hours at it, working on a stock investment program.

On-the-Job Behaviors

Once hired, Gary seemed to work well within the department. He was quiet and reserved, but the other employees liked him right from the start. In many respects, he was a calming influence, balancing the outspoken and sometimes abrasive work style of another staff member in the department. He could always find something good to say about someone or something, delivering his comments in a wry, understated way that made people smile and even laugh. His comments would sometimes throw the other person off guard and would help reveal the funny side of an issue. If a misunderstanding arose between two staff members, Gary was the one who could usually smooth things over.

The head of technical services, Dorothy, could count on Gary to do his tasks accurately. However, she soon discovered that Gary would find what he thought was a better or faster way to handle a task and make the change on his own. He did not realize that if he changed what he was doing, another departmental member's handling of the same item would be affected.

Action Plan

Once she was aware of this pattern, Dorothy spoke with Gary about these changes. As an action plan, Dorothy suggested that Gary keep handy a copy of the written steps in the processing of an item and check off each step as he completed it according to the instructions. Once the checking-off of the step was done, she asked Gary not to go back over that particular step again. This action plan also stated that Gary would bring his suggestions to Dorothy for consideration. Gary followed this action plan and refrained from making any changes affecting departmental work flow until he had spoken with his supervisor.

Departmental Work Flow

Meanwhile, Dorothy announced to her staff that recently she had been informed by the director that within the next two months her department would be receiving a large shipment of books to be added to the collection. Special funds had been found to purchase a private collection that would enhance a specific subject collection in the library. To meet the library's commitment, all the books would have to be cataloged and processed within the year.

Mid-year Review

At Gary's mid-year review, he expressed concerns to Dorothy about errors occurring throughout the technical services procedures that slowed down the entire process. Dorothy asked for examples and Gary indicated some possible problems with the current work flow (not with the persons doing the processing). It was obvious to Dorothy that Gary had been mulling over in his mind how to improve the speed of the processing without sacrificing accuracy. She also was impressed by how he had analyzed the situation and had thought it through before discussing it with her. After Gary and Dorothy talked, they agreed it would be beneficial to examine the entire process of adding a book to pinpoint any steps contributing to delays. Gary's suggestions were timely; the looming prospect of adding a large number of books to the collection was making the technical services staff anxious about the impending increase in the work load.

Project to Improve Work Flow

With Dorothy's approval, over the next several weeks Gary spent a few hours each week reviewing with other departmental members the number and types of steps in processing a newly received book. Dorothy was pleased to see that, once Gary started on this project, he concentrated on fulfilling his regular duties more quickly so that he would have sufficient time to work on the project. He asked to stay later one or two times to work undisturbed on diagramming the process. More important, he would actually help other staff members with their work while he was learning exactly how they did a procedure.

After several weeks, Gary presented a flowchart of the steps involved in processing a new book from receiving to cataloging, to adding barcodes, to applying labels and security strips, to adding the bibliographic record to the database. He highlighted the critical and the more time-consuming steps. Using this chart at the next three departmental meetings, Dorothy and her technical services staff brainstormed ways to eliminate or combine steps and to add "checkpoints" to ensure accuracy.

Gary's Skills Exhibited

Throughout Gary's work on the project and the subsequent departmental discussion based on his charts, Dorothy was very surprised by the tact and skill Gary exhibited. Because normally Gary was quiet and self-effacing, Dorothy previously had no idea of the analytical skills he possessed. He could see the overall process, but also break its components into manageable and logical steps that were clear to the other technical services staff. Dorothy observed Gary while he was gathering the information for the project and then explaining the results during the departmental meetings. Even in sometimes difficult or tense discussions on how work currently was being done and what changes might be made to improve the work flow, Gary's thoughtful comments and objective, quiet voice helped immensely to smooth over disagreements and dissension.

With Gary's assistance, the technical services staff agreed to change several procedures. Two changes were controversial—not everyone agreed that the "new" way would be an improvement. Before the discussion got heated to the point where those staff opposed would not be willing to back down, Gary tactfully suggested that the changes be implemented in phases to test the results and then make any needed modifications. That compromise worked, and eventually all the changes were made without further discord.

Benefits to Service

This project had several benefits for the department. The processing time for getting a book from receipt to the shelf improved. Staff who were feeling a bit panicked about the deadline for processing the special large collection now felt that the department could handle this major project. Part of that feeling of confidence came from the knowledge they had gained about how each of them contributed to the entire process.

A side benefit for Dorothy was that she became aware of Gary's strengths. Her end-of-the-year evaluation of him reflects her recognition of his skills. She is now able to set goals for Gary that will further enhance the contributions he can make to the department and the library.

JOB DESCRIPTION
TECHNICAL SERVICES ASSISTANT

Position Title	Assistant, Technical Services
Reports to	Head, Technical Services
Category	Clerical
Grade	Level 1 or above
Classification	Part-time, nonexempt or Full-time, nonexempt
Responsibility	To support through clerical activity the daily routines of the technical services department while demonstrating accuracy and efficiency in assigned duties.

Duties

*1. Automated bibliographic utility duties to include:

—search database and print edit sheets,

—enter information into database according to the format designated cataloger,

—operate computer printers,

—perform other computer-related, database maintenance activities.

*2. Automated system cataloging duties to include:

—support database authority work,

—change, correct, and update database,

—merge bibliographic records,

—delete and add bibliographic records to database,

—generate reports.

*3. Barcode, label, and process adult and juvenile print and nonprint materials.

*4. Perform brief cataloging and processing for the paperback book collections.

*Indicates essential functions of this position.

*5. Perform clerical duties required to maintain departmental records to include:

   –filing and/or alphabetizing,

   –preparing lists,

   –stamping materials,

   –ordering.

6. Perform other related duties as required.

*Indicates essential functions of this position.

Authority   Does not supervise other employees but performs under direct authority of Head, Technical Services.

Experience and Education Required

1. At the high school graduate level or above, ability to alphabetize, to put numbers in order, and to read and comprehend both written and oral instructions, and to respond appropriately is required.

2. Proficiency in the application of basic clerical skills and the ability to process information effectively using a computer required.

3. Practical library experience received from either paid or volunteer involvement highly desirable but is not required.

4. Pleasant and courteous telephone response is required.

5. Physical strength and dexterity are required to handle informational items and boxes up to 25 pounds in weight, and to transport loaded book carts; physical ability to put items in order on high and low shelves is also required.

PERFORMANCE APPRAISAL

NAME (last, first):	Gary	DATE: 10/31/XX
POSITION:	Technical Services Assistant	
SUPERVISOR:	Head, Technical Services	
BEGAN EMPLOYMENT:	1/15/XX	

The Standards of Performance system is based on the principle that an employee must know the expectations of the job and that the supervisor will inform the employee of how he or she is performing according to those expectations.

The supervisor will discuss this report with the employee and, if needed, will assist in developing an action plan for improvement.

In signing this report, the employee acknowledges having had the opportunity to review and discuss the performance appraisal, not necessarily that he or she is in agreement with the conclusions.

Upon completion and signature by employee and supervisor, this report is reviewed and signed by the Library Director.

Only the last three annual performance appraisals are kept active for review.

GUIDELINES FOR EVALUATION

- The Code of Service expresses the overall philosophy of service for Rocky River Public Library. The Code is the foundation upon which the Standards of Performance are built.

- The Standards of Performance are the types of behavior expected of an employee necessary to achieve the intent of the Code of Service.

- The Standards of Performance apply to daily performance. Throughout the year the supervisor regularly will evaluate, based on the Standards, the employee's performance.

- Effective evaluation is based on an employee's continuing pattern of behavior. Evaluation for any Standard of Performance is not based on single, unrelated actions.

- Evaluation of an employee is ongoing. When a supervisor perceives that an employee is having difficulty meeting a Standard of Performance, the supervisor is obligated to discuss with the employee what action is needed to meet the standard. The supervisor and the employee decide on the time and resources needed to meet the standard.

- For evaluation, the supervisor must document, with examples of specific, observed actions, any pattern of continuing behavior which either falls into the category of "needs improvement" (NI) or "exceeds standard" (ES). If an employee "meets standard" (MS), the supervisor has the option of either documenting or not.

- In order for an employee to receive an overall "meets standards" or "exceeds the standards that employee must have at least a 2.0 at point B2 on the tabulation sheet. This performance would reflect a level of at least "meets standards" for the employee's position responsibilities.

- Every employee's evaluation is reviewed by the Director, with the option of review by the Deputy Director.

- The employee's compensation is related directly to the employee's evaluation. The overall pattern of the evaluation determines the employee's level of compensation.

- The employee always has both the right and the responsibility to discuss with his or her immediate supervisor any disparity between the employee's interpretation of his or her behavior and the supervisor's interpretation. If the employee and the supervisor cannot come to a mutually agreeable plan of action, the Director is the final arbiter.

PERFORMANCE STANDARDS

A. Service to Patrons and Coworkers	
1. *Makes eye contact, greets others sincerely, and speaks in a friendly manner.*	ES

Comments

Throughout this year, you have resolved departmental disagreements with humor and tact, often in difficult situations which could have led to wide-spread contention.

Examples of Behavior

On several occasions I have observed you step in and calm down two "sparring" coworkers, thus stopping minor disagreements from growing into major ones (e.g., 3/36; 4/11; 6/10; 8/14; 9/22). During the project of charting the steps in processing a book, you effectively used your interpersonal skills to diffuse sensitive issues.

Action Plan

2. *Welcomes and serves without regard to race, color, religion, gender, sexual preference, national origin, disability, age, ancestry, or other characteristics.*	MS

Comments

You exhibit respect for all coworkers.

Examples of Behavior

Action Plan

3. *Acknowledges a patron's presence immediately, even if occupied.*

NA

Comments

Examples of Behavior

Action Plan

4. *Does not spend an undue amount of time or effort with one patron if another patron is waiting.*

NA

Comments

Examples of Behavior

Action Plan

A.	**Service to Patrons and Coworkers** (continued)	

5. *Takes personal responsibility for meeting patron and staff needs correctly (informational and physical access to materials).*   ES

   Comments

   On your own, you devised a workable plan to improve the processing time of books, thus increasing access.

   Examples of Behavior

   You presented a workable plan to chart the processing of a book from receipt to shelf-readiness in order to pinpoint areas of delay. With my approval, you did appropriate interviewing of staff to represent the various steps accurately. You highlighted problem areas for discussion. This in-depth project, lasting more than two months, demonstrated your initiative and analytical skills. On several occasions you have offered your assistance to coworkers stuck with a computer-related problem.

   Action Plan

6. *Does not communicate any value judgment when interacting with a patron.*   NA

   Comments

   Examples of Behavior

   Action Plan

7. *Verifies with the patron or coworker that his or her needs have been met.*	MS
Comments	
Examples of Behavior	
Action Plan	

8. *Implements appropriate use of technology.*	MS
Comments	
This year you have learned technology needed for your duties. Also, you have demonstrated both an ease in working with your coworkers and a personal comfort level with computers. I would like to see you develop your computer skills so that you become the computer resource person in our department. The library can support your growth in this area through additional training.	
Examples of Behavior	
Action Plan	

	A. **Service to Patrons and Coworkers** (continued)	
	9. *Exhibits proper telephone use and etiquette.*	MS

Comments

You are knowledgeable about the features of the telephone system and use the phone in a courteous and efficient manner.

Examples of Behavior

Action Plan

---

	10. *Exhibits a cooperative team spirit.*	ES

Comments

You work actively to blend differing work styles of coworkers into a departmental team.

Examples of Behavior

Throughout the year I have noted (see standard A1) many occasions when by your behavior and example you have smoothed over differences in the department. The project you initiated and conducted on charting the delays in processing a book helped staff see how to improve what they were doing. You promote cooperation through your comments and actions. You work actively to demonstrate to your coworkers how they each contribute to the processing of an item.

Action Plan

11. *Puts service above any personal activities or interests while on duty.*

ES

Comments

I have never observed you conducting personal business during scheduled work hours.

Examples of Behavior

Even for personal business which takes a short period of time, you always use personal time.

Action Plan

12. *Is ready for duty at/during scheduled times.*

MS

Comments

You consistently are at your work station when scheduled. You offered to stay late two times to work on your project.

Examples of Behavior

Action Plan

A.	**Service to Patrons and Coworkers** (continued)	

13. *Is attentive to others' complaints and, when applicable, refers the complaints to the appropriate level.* MS

Comments

You are consistent in informing me, your supervisor, of possible areas of complaint from other staff. I encourage you to continue to think of possible options for resolving these areas of concern and offer them to me and the department for discussion (as you did with charting the delays in book processing).

Examples of Behavior

Action Plan

14. *Takes responsibility for learning updated internal procedures.* MS

Comments

You stay current with departmental and library-wide procedures.

Examples of Behavior

Action Plan

| 15. *Upholds library policies and established procedures.* | MS |

15. *Upholds library policies and established procedures.*

Comments

You follow established procedures.

Examples of Behavior

Action Plan

16. *Upholds the intellectual freedom of the patron.*

NA

Comments

Examples of Behavior

Action Plan

A. **Service to Patrons and Coworkers** (continued)	
17. *Upholds all confidentiality rights of the patron.*	MS
Comments	
You do not display or discuss patron or staff personal information available in the automated system's database.	
Examples of Behavior	
Action Plan	

B.	**Personal Development**	
	1. *Plans own time to meet obligations and specified deadlines.*	ES
	Comments	
	You have finished your assigned tasks on time and have been able to take on an additional major responsibility.	
	Examples of Behavior	
	In addition to your regular duties, you completed the major project of charting the processing of a book through all the technical services steps. This project took several weeks. While working on this project, you helped your coworkers in the completion of several of their tasks (e.g., the checking in of a large order of books; the return of damaged books to the book jobber; the labeling of the computer software programs).	
	Action Plan	
	2. *Actively listens to supervisor and accepts direction, seeking further advice from the supervisor as needed.*	ES
	Comments	
	You offer workable suggestions for the work you are doing.	
	Examples of Behavior	
	Examples of suggestions for simplification and faster processing offered by you: the "batching" of recently requested reserve items for faster processing; verification of duplicate holdings titles by a technical services assistant rather than the cataloger; checking first to see if a reference title is new or an updated edition to avoid delays in processing.	
	Action Plan	

B. **Personal Development** (continued)	
3. *Accepts responsibility for own actions and obligations.*	ES
Comments	
You accept constructive criticism and then apply corrective steps for improvement.	
Examples of Behavior	
You took to heart my suggestions for fitting change into an overall departmental work flow, and built upon the idea by analyzing a department-wide process (see standards A5 and B2).	
Action Plan	
4. *Adapts to change.*	ES
Comments	
You actively assist your coworkers in adjusting to changes that affect them.	
Examples of Behavior	
You have been a strong advocate of changes in the department's procedures to improve efficiency and accuracy. At the same time, you have actively promoted the changes in a manner that is sensitive to the fears and concerns of your coworkers. The way you offer compromises and give insights into the benefits of the changes have helped your coworkers adjust to the changes that affect them.	
Action Plan	

5. *Uses library-provided means for continuing education or training.*	MS

Comments

Examples of Behavior

Action Plan

6. *Communicates clearly and honestly.*	ES

Comments

You communicate effectively with your coworkers in difficult and sensitive situations.

Examples of Behavior

See standard A1 for examples.

Action Plan

B.	**Personal Development** (continued)	
	7. *Demonstrates appropriate initiative within a team framework.*	ES

Comments

You presented a workable plan to improve the processing of books and provide faster and more accurate access to the collections.

Examples of Behavior

Throughout the year you have offered suggestions for improving access to the collections through faster processing of materials and elimination of errors. These suggestions were consistently made in the context of the staff working together to make needed changes. See examples in A5 and B2.

Action Plan

C.	**Specific Job Standards**	
	Items under this category relate directly to the individual's position description.	
	1. Perform automated bibliographic utility database duties which include: —search database and print edit sheets; —enter information into database; —operate computer printers; —perform database maintenance activities	ES

Comments

You have a thorough knowledge of the cataloging utility and automated cataloging module.

Examples of Behavior

You use your knowledge to brainstorm with your coworkers improvements in technical services processes. Your contributions to improving efficiency and accuracy are highlighted in standards A5 and B2.

Action Plan

	2. Perform automated system cataloging duties which include: —support database authority work; —change, correct, and update database; —merge bibliographic records; —delete and add bibliographic records; —generate reports	ES

Comments

See standard B1.

Examples of Behavior

See standard B1.

Action Plan

C.	**Specific Job Standards** (continued) *Items under this category relate directly to the individual's position description.*	
	3. Barcode, label, and process adult and juvenile print and nonprint materials.	MS
	Comments You accurately process print materials.	
	Examples of Behavior	
	Action Plan	
	4. Perform brief cataloging and processing for the paperback book collections.	ES
	Comments Your work is accurate and efficient, resulting in a shortening of the time from receipt to the shelf.	
	Examples of Behavior You have contributed valuable ideas and suggestions for improving the processing of paperbacks (e.g., the handling of duplicate holdings; the streamlining of the cataloging).	
	Action Plan	

Items under this category relate directly to the individual's position description.

5. Package and process the CD-ROM and software collections. | MS

Comments

Examples of Behavior

Action Plan

Comments by Supervisor

Your strong analytical skills are a valuable asset to our department. You are able to see how the various steps in the processing of an item fit into the overall work flow of the department. Your tact and humor help you translate your suggestions and ideas for procedural changes into a workable plan which is accepted by your coworkers. A major project which you initiated and accomplished not only helped our department handle a large collection of additional titles, but also was a catalyst for ongoing departmental discussion on ways to continue to streamline our processes.

You know the automated cataloging module very well. I encourage you to take a training workshop this coming year and work with me in training new staff or in offering "refresher" training for your coworkers.

Overall Action Plan

_____

Employee's signature   Date

_____

Supervisor's signature   Date

_____

Reviewer's signature   Date

Recommended for Level: _____

Comments by Employee

Thank you for your kind comments. My coworkers have been an immense help to me—I have learned by working with them. I don't know if I could be a trainer—but it sounds like an interesting challenge, and I am willing to try.

_____
Employee's signature   Date

_____
Supervisor's signature   Date

_____
Reviewer's signature   Date

ES = 3 points; MS = 2 points; NI = 1 point
Round all numbers to the nearest "tenth" at each step of the calculation
(except B2)—Examples: 2.41 = 2.4 and 2.75 = 2.8.

1. Determine the total number of applicable standards for each:

Service: _13_
Personal Development: _7_

Total above two categories: _20_ (A)

Specific Job Standards: _5_
Supervisory: _0_

Total above two categories: _5_ (B)

2. Determine point value for each of the applicable sections:

Service:
number of ES x 3 = _12_ number of MS x 2 = _18_ number of NI = _0_
Total for Service Standards: _30_

Personal Development:
number of ES x 3 = _18_ number of MS x 2 = _2_ number of NI = _0_
Total for Personal Development: _20_

Grand total of above two categories: _50_ (A1)

Specific Job Standards:
number of ES x 3 = _9_ number of MS x 2 = _4_ number of NI = _0_
Total for Specific Job Standards: _13_

Supervisory:
number of ES x 3 = _0_ number of MS x 2 = _0_ number of NI = _0_
Total for Supervisory Standards: _0_

Grand total of above two categories: _13_ (B1)

3. To determine the overall point value for Service and Development sections:

   Take **A1** _50_ and divide by **A** _20_

   This results in **A2**: _2.5_ (the value for these sections)

4. To determine overall point value for the specific Job Standards and Supervisors:

   Take **B1** _13_ and divide by **B** _5_

   This results in **B2**: _2.6_* (the value for these sections)

   > *** B2:**
   > **Must be 2.0 or higher to proceed with calculation.**

5. To determine overall point value for this evaluation:

   Add **A2** _2.5_ to **B2** _2.6_ This results in **B3**: _5.1_

   Now divide **B3** by 2 _2.6_ This is the total point value for this evaluation

   Using this number, the **overall evaluation** is rated _ES_

ES	= 2.5 or higher
MS3	= 2.4–2.2
MS2	= 2.1–1.8
MS1	= 1.7–1.5
NI	= 1.4 or lower

Employee's name: _____

Supervisor's signature: _____

Date: _____

APPENDIX A

Code of Service

The Code of Service is the foundation upon which the performance appraisal system is based. It is the document approved by the policy-making board of the library, the Board of Library Trustees. It applies to all staff within the library.

CODE OF SERVICE

Rocky River Public Library

- The library public is entitled to easily accessible library collections in a safe, clean, organized, and appropriate environment staffed with friendly, courteous people.

- Each member of the library public is to be welcomed, fairly and courteously, without discrimination.

- Service to the public takes precedence over the library's internal paperwork and internal communications.

- Information given to the library public will be based on verifiable, current sources, clearly communicated, and given in a timely manner.

Approved by the Board of Library Trustees
December 8, 19XX

Standards of Performance Guidelines

The Standards of Performance Guidelines are the key to ensuring that all supervisors within the library are evaluating staff according to the same levels of performance. The examples of behavior for "meets standard," "exceeds standard," and "needs improvement" indicate the level for each.

Supervisors use their own words and comments in the actual evaluation of an employee, using the Guidelines only for determining the "meets," "exceeds," or "needs improvement" levels.

These comments have been written by the supervisory staff to give all employees examples of the types of behavior that are expected for the Standards of Performance. These examples will be used by supervisors as guidelines when writing comments specific to the employee. The wording for the comments will vary for each employee.

The comments written by the supervisor will conform to the performance levels as indicated below.

Meets Standard (MS)
Consistently performs at a satisfactory level.

Exceeds Standard (ES)
Substantially exceeds the standard consistently with little or no prompting.

Needs Improvement (NI)
Often does not meet the standard. Needs action plan to improve.

A. | Service to Patrons and Coworkers

1. **Makes eye contact, greets others sincerely, and speaks in a friendly manner.**

    MS   You greet all patrons and coworkers politely.
    You immediately look up when patrons or coworkers approach and greet them warmly.
    You recognize frequent patrons.
    You speak in a friendly manner to all staff.

    ES   You maintain a consistently friendly manner with difficult patrons or staff.
    You are able to acknowledge and carry on a friendly conversation with most of the patrons with whom you have contact.

    NI   You are frequently unpleasant (e.g., you rarely smile; you have an abrupt manner; you make someone feel he or she is annoying you).
    You do not look up when someone approaches you.
    You only occasionally smile and make eye contact.
    You are pleasant only to people you like or know.

2. **Welcomes and serves without regard to race, color, religion, gender, sexual preference, national origin, disability, age, ancestry, or other characteristics.**

    MS   You welcome and serve all patrons equally.
    You exhibit respect for all patrons.
    You welcome and work with all coworkers without prejudice.
    You exhibit respect for all coworkers.

    ES   You have taken the initiative to learn appropriate service techniques to serve _____ [e.g., disabled] patrons more effectively.
    You go out of your way to help coworkers blend into the organization.
    You are a resource person on the operation of equipment to serve the disabled (e.g., TTY).
    You offer valid suggestions for resources to add to the collections to meet the needs of an underserved population in the community.

    NI   You ignore or avoid helping _____ [e.g., older people; young adults; Middle Eastern patrons].
    You give substandard service to _____ [e.g., young adults].
    You are rude to _____ [e.g., children].
    You avoid helping _____ [e.g., student shelvers].

A. **Service to Patrons and Coworkers** (continued)

3. **Acknowledges a patron's presence immediately, even if occupied.**

   MS   Even if busy with another patron, you will indicate to a waiting patron by voice or manner that someone will help them as soon as possible.

   You consistently are aware of patrons needing assistance.

   You immediately end conversations with other staff members when a patron approaches.

   ES   While very busy with serving patrons, you consistently put waiting patrons at ease without irritating the patrons you are currently helping.

   When you encounter a waiting patron, even if you are "off the floor," you consistently go out of your way to assist.

   When you encounter a waiting patron, even if you are not a staff member of the department in which the patron is waiting, you consistently go out of your way to assist.

   NI   You are so preoccupied with what you are doing, you do not notice a patron who needs assistance.

   You rarely address a patron until you end your conversation with a staff member.

   You interrupt a conversation with a staff member only to inform a patron that you will be with them shortly, then you finish the conversation.

4. **Does not spend an undue amount of time or effort with one patron if another patron is waiting.**

   MS   You successfully juggle the demands of patrons needing assistance at the same time.

   ES   When service activity is extraordinarily high, you are able to calmly and easily handle many patrons' demands without a significant loss in service quality.

   NI   You ignore a patron waiting for assistance if you are busy helping another patron.

   You abruptly stop helping a patron if another patron seeks assistance.

5. **Takes personal responsibility for meeting patron and staff needs correctly (informational and physical access to materials).**

MS   You are able to answer general questions relating to other service departments.

You never hesitate to ask another staff member for assistance if you are unable to answer a question.

You cite sources of information given to a patron.

When appropriate, you contact sources outside the library or provide a reasonable referral.

You assist patrons and staff who ask for help in physically accessing materials.

You display a positive and helpful attitude to any request for physical assistance to accessing materials.

You ask patrons and staff with special physical needs whether they need assistance.

ES   You have taken the initiative to learn _____ [e.g., microfilm reader/printer; operation of the public copier] which is not part of your job description to the extent you are able to assist if asked.

You demonstrate creativity and initiative in finding answers or solutions to difficult requests.

You consistently identify alternative sources or resources for use by staff, when appropriate (e.g., listing what libraries have IBM computers for public use; researching other libraries for a more efficient way of processing materials).

You devise a workable plan to improve physical access to materials.

NI   You are unable to answer general questions relating to another service department.

You often resent offers of help from coworkers in answering difficult questions.

You do not provide guidance for patrons to the proper source or department when needed.

You seldom cite sources of information given to a patron.

You grudgingly help to improve physical access to materials.

You fail to ask for help, if needed, to improve physical access to materials.

You are reluctant to help a coworker when you have the needed answer to a question or problem.

Service to Patrons and Coworkers (continued)

6. **Does not communicate any value judgment when interacting with a patron.**

    MS You provide assistance without communicating any value judgment.
    You do not make any value comments about patrons where they can be heard
    by other patrons.

    ES You do not communicate any negative judgment pertaining to any patron at
    any time.

    NI You offer unsolicited negative comments to patrons (e.g., "That's a dumb
    question;" "Why did you pick that book? It's awful.").

7. **Verifies with the patron or coworker that his or her needs have been met.**

    MS After assisting someone, you verify that his or her needs have been met.
    You rephrase the request to be sure both patron or coworker and you are in
    agreement as to what is needed.

    ES You consistently check with the patron before he or she has left the building to
    verify he or she has found the information requested.
    You consistently follow through with coworkers to determine whether the
    assistance you provided was useful.
    If the assistance you provided a coworker was not useful, you persist in
    helping the coworker until a successful resolution is found.

    NI You seldom ask a patron if he or she has found what is needed.
    You take patrons to the shelves and leave them immediately.
    You seldom rephrase the request to be sure you and the patron or coworker
    are in agreement as to what is needed.
    After providing assistance to a coworker, you seldom check that the assistance
    met the coworker's need.
    You do not make the effort to verify what your coworkers need; you
    consequently provide inadequate assistance.

8. **Implements appropriate use of technology.**

MS You learn technology needed for your duties.
You keep up-to-date on automated catalog techniques useful for your position.
You learn, in an appropriate period of time, skills for using new technology.

ES Other staff consistently turn to you for help with technology, even though training on technology is not part of your regular duties.
Though not part of your job description, you are a resource person for staff to learn about new technology.
On your own, you continually learn about new technology-related techniques or functions that help you serve the public or staff more effectively.
You are proficient in using several modules of the automated system, knowledge of which is not normally part of your job, to serve the public or your coworkers more efficiently.

NI You refuse to learn technology useful for serving the public or your coworkers.
You do not keep up-to-date with training provided for new technology.
You avoid using technology to help the public or your coworkers.
You are not able or willing to offer relevant assistance for the public using technology.

9. **Exhibits proper telephone use and etiquette.**

MS You efficiently answer calls and direct them to the proper department.
You do not allow calls to remain on hold for longer than necessary.
You properly distinguish between incoming and intercom calls.
You know how to pick up a call from another telephone in a group.
You are knowledgeable about the features of the telephone system.

ES The knowledge, courtesy, and responsiveness you exhibit on the telephone set an exemplary standard for others.
You train others in the proper operation of the telephone.
You are a resource person whom staff turn to when they are unsure about the operation of the telephone.

NI You often neglect to check back for calls on hold.
You do not get enough information from a caller, often causing unnecessary transfers.
You are rude to callers.
You frequently "cut off" incoming calls.
You frequently pick up wrong lines.
You consistently cannot distinguish between an intercom and an incoming call.

10. Exhibits a cooperative team spirit.

MS   You exhibit a cooperative team spirit by assisting others or requesting assistance of others as the situation warrants.

You handle conflicts created by differences in work style or personality with courtesy and fairness.

You cheerfully assist a coworker in finding a solution to a problem.

You offer suggestions or alternatives when needed.

You tactfully clarified a specific point when you observed misinformation being given by a coworker.

ES   You take a lead in promoting cooperation and uplifting the spirits of coworkers.

You consistently are flexible when scheduling must be changed unexpectedly.

You work actively to blend differing work styles of coworkers into a departmental work force.

You consistently assist coworkers by finding creative and innovative solutions to difficult problems.

You offer assistance or instruction to improve coworkers' skills.

NI   You tend to work as a separate and distinct individual, rarely assisting others or requesting assistance of others as situations warrant.

You do not take part in staff meetings or department meetings.

You display frequent unwillingness to compromise with coworkers who practice different work styles.

You often refuse to assist fellow staff members (e.g., saying "That's not my job").

You frequently grumble when a coworker asks for assistance.

You rudely interrupt a coworker's conversation with a patron to flatly state that the coworker is wrong.

11. Puts service above any personal activities or interests while on duty.

MS   You consistently put service to the public above any personal activities or interests.

ES   You do not conduct personal business during scheduled work hours.

NI   You seldom put service to the public above any personal activities or interests while on duty.

You put personal activities or interests above service to the public while on
duty (e.g., photocopying recipes or bills, looking up personal medical
information, or making plans for an after-work get-together during
scheduled work hours).

12. Is ready for duty at/during scheduled times.

MS   You consistently are at your service position when scheduled.

ES   You consistently recognize and acknowledge service needs by willingly
adjusting your work time (e.g., coming in earlier or staying later).

NI   You frequently are not at your service position when scheduled.
You prepare to leave during your scheduled work time.

**13. Is attentive to others' complaints and, when applicable, refers the complaints to the
appropriate level.**

MS   You receive a complaint with dignity, poise, and an open mind.
You understand and correctly use the library's Collection Development Policy.
You inform a supervisor of a complaint within a working day.
If applicable, you inform the complainant of the policy concerning the
complaint.

ES   You inform a supervisor of flaws within the physical environment which might
lead to a complaint.
You notify a supervisor of areas of the collection particularly vulnerable to
complaint and offer options or solutions.
You consistently assist your supervisor with recognition of actions or decisions
which have potential to create complaints, and offer feasible alternatives.

NI   You neglect to inform your supervisor of a complaint.
You fail to ask for help when unsure how to handle a complaint.
You encourage nonproductive grousing among your coworkers.

A. Service to Patrons and Coworkers (continued)

14. Takes responsibility for learning updated internal procedures.

MS You attend meetings regularly.
If you are not sure about a procedure, you make it a point to get the correct information.
You read minutes of meetings, memos, and e-mail.
You are current with organizational safety procedures and are able to immediately locate the departmental safety manual.

ES You immediately alert the appropriate person of safety concerns and follow through with solutions or implementations of procedures.
You take the initiative to inform coworkers of changes in procedures when you observe that updated procedures are not being followed.
Other staff consistently look to you for answers on updated procedures.
You are actively involved in development of or training in safety and security matters.

NI You are not informed about the activities in your department.
You do not read memos or e-mail regularly.
You are unaware of organizational safety procedures and may not remember where to locate the departmental safety manual.

15. Upholds library policies and established procedures.

MS You accept written policies and enforce their use.
You do not communicate negative attitudes on established library policy in front of patrons.
You follow established procedures.
You understand and enforce the Statement on User Behavior.
You apply the Statement on User Behavior equally to all patrons.
You do not publicly challenge other staff members' applications of the Statement on User Behavior.
You communicate policy or procedural concerns first to your supervisor.
You follow safety and security procedures.

ES You adhere to policies and attempt to present the most positive aspects of the policy when faced with a difficult patron.
You calmly and efficiently enforce the Statement on User Behavior in difficult or threatening situations.
You communicate policy or procedural concerns first to a supervisor and offer feasible suggestions for revision.

NI   You are openly critical of approved library policies (e.g., saying "This is a stupid rule" in front of patrons; changing the rules per individual patron).

You criticize the library's policy or procedure in a subtle way (e.g., "I don't know why they do it this way").

You are critical of library policies to other staff members when or where you can be overheard by patrons.

You deviate from established procedure without just cause (e.g., issuing checks on Friday instead of Tuesday).

You single out a certain group for more rigorous enforcement of the Statement on User Behavior.

You rarely enforce the Statement on User Behavior.

You share policy or procedural concerns only with nonsupervisory coworkers.

You bypass your supervisor when expressing policy or procedural concerns.

You do not follow safety or security procedures.

16. Upholds the intellectual freedom of the patron.

MS   You assist patrons without questioning reasons for needing specified information.

You attempt to select material on both sides of controversial issues.

ES   You significantly enhance your or others' understanding of intellectual freedom issues through attending workshops, reading articles, sharing information gathered.

NI   You frequently question patrons as to why information is required.

In material selection, you reject material that doesn't support your own viewpoint.

17. Upholds all confidentiality rights of the patron.

MS   You do not discuss a patron's personal or borrowing information with staff members or other patrons.

You do not leave or display any patron's personal or borrowing information where it can be viewed by others.

ES   You are actively involved in training staff on confidentiality.

You actively work towards preventing or correcting breaches of confidentiality by others.

NI   You frequently look at patrons' personal information (i.e., address, age, list of items checked out) and discuss this information with others.

You use a patron's personal information for your personal use (e.g., getting a phone number of a patron you want to contact for personal reasons).

Personal Development

1. **Plans own time to meet obligations and specified deadlines.**

   MS   You meet your obligations on time—correctly and efficiently.

   ES   You completed your assignments on time and were able to assume additional assignments.
   Having fulfilled your own deadlines, you offer assistance to others who might need help in fulfilling their deadline commitments.

   NI   You frequently miss set deadlines.
   You do not communicate an impending missed deadline with those to be affected.
   You do not plan your time effectively.

2. **Actively listens to supervisor and accepts direction, seeking further advice from the supervisor as needed.**

   MS   You accept direction.
   You ask for further advice when needed.

   ES   You offer workable suggestions when you see a better way of accomplishing the task given to you.

   NI   You frequently do not accept direction.
   You fail to ask for further clarification if instructions are unclear to you.

3. **Accepts responsibility for own actions and obligations.**

   MS   You admit to your mistakes.
   You accept constructive criticism.

   ES   When you make a mistake, you make a responsible effort to correct it.
   You accept constructive criticism, seeking clarification and suggestions for improvement which you then apply.

   NI   You do not admit your mistakes.
   You do not accept constructive criticism.

4. **Adapts to change.**

MS You follow new policies and procedures.
   You adjust to changes in the work environment.

ES You actively assist users and staff in adjusting to changes that affect them.

NI Your resistance to change is disruptive.
   You do not learn new policies and procedures.

5. **Uses library-provided means for continuing education or training.**

MS You attend workshops, seminars, or training suited for your position.
   You express a positive attitude towards mandatory attendance programs, such as Staff Day.

ES You incorporate pertinent information and skills into your job performance, and actively share information with coworkers without prompting.

NI You resist or refuse to attend workshops, seminars, or training suited for your position.
   You are unreceptive to mandatory attendance programs, such as Staff Day.

6. **Communicates clearly and honestly.**

MS You communicate effectively for the needs of your position.
   You do not hesitate to ask questions or seek clarification, when needed.

ES You communicate effectively in difficult or sensitive situations.
   You defuse confrontational situations using your communication skills.

NI You are often unclear or imprecise when communicating with others.
   You are often uncommunicative or deliberately deceptive.
   You refuse to ask questions or seek clarification, when needed.

7. **Demonstrates appropriate initiative within a team framework.**

MS You step in to help a coworker, when needed, to avoid disrupting service.
   When you finish your assigned duties, you automatically start another task without being told.

B. **Personal Development** (continued)

    ES   You present a workable plan to improve service.

    NI   You arbitrarily take on another employee's duties when your own are not completed.
You decide to _____ [e.g., change a display] without first okaying it with those involved.
When you finish your assigned duties, you stand around saying you are bored.

C. **Specific Job Standards**

Comments under this category relate directly to the performance of the work as outlined in the job description.

D. **Supervisory Standards**

1. **Establishes cooperation and communication among staff.**

    MS   You treat staff fairly.
You solicit staff involvement in the decision-making process.
You listen with an open mind and keep staff informed.

    ES   You foster an effective team effort.
You encourage and promote effective staff involvement in improving productivity and service.

    NI   You are closed-minded and unwilling to accept staff input.
You are authoritative and unyielding with staff.

2. **Makes appropriate decisions.**

    MS   Your decisions are well considered.
You make timely decisions.

    ES   You consistently make reliable decisions in difficult or sensitive situations.

    NI   You make decisions without sufficient information.
You put off making decisions.
You waffle.

3. **Resolves problems fairly.**

MS   You use a cooperative, nonautocratic style.
You do whatever you can to get problems worked out as soon as possible.
You ask for help if you cannot resolve a problem.
You are willing to help others with a problem if you are knowledgeable in that area.

ES   Once a problem is resolved, you investigate what caused it and prevent it from occurring again through corrective action.

NI   You do not try to work with others to help solve problems.
You will complain to others about problems, but not take steps to try and resolve them.

4. **Effectively and fairly manages the work flow of staff.**

MS   You clearly relate instructions for performing assigned tasks and freely answer any questions.
You make sure duties are assigned according to time and availability of workers.
You delegate responsibly.

ES   You design and implement procedures that increase staff effectiveness.
You develop the potential of your staff through the management of work flow.

NI   You are not precise when giving instructions for performance of job duties.
You do not communicate changes to procedures clearly, or at all, thus impeding efficiency and performance.
You do not delegate work, attempting to do much of it yourself.

5. **Enforces all policies and work procedures fairly.**

MS   You enforce all policies and work procedures fairly.

ES   You communicate the implications and rationale of policies and procedures, anticipating and handling successfully the concerns of staff.

NI   You tend not to enforce all policies and work procedures fairly _____ [e.g., by showing favoritism, discrimination, bias].

D. **Supervisory Standards** (continued)

6. **Effectively and fairly manages resources.**

   MS   You plan ahead, organizing your resources to meet your responsibilities.
   You manage priorities according to available resources.
   You schedule staff with consideration for both the library and the individual.

   ES   Your management of resources results in savings of time or money for the
   library.
   You are highly resourceful in using your staff and equipment to the best
   advantage.

   NI   You seldom plan ahead, causing confusion.
   You do not plan according to your budget.
   You frequently do not plan _____ [e.g., your department's activities].

7. **Works effectively with staff to improve performance.**

   MS   You meet regularly (at least quarterly) with each member of your department.
   You provide resources and scheduling for attendance at workshops or
   conferences.
   You offer praise, not just criticism.

   ES   You develop training and development programs for staff.
   You continually develop ways for your staff to learn new skills.

   NI   You seldom meet with your staff.
   You are inconsistent in who or who does not receive attention to performance.
   You do not permit those you supervise to attend workshops or classes.

8. **Documents performance, then evaluates staff objectively and constructively, and in a timely manner.**

   MS   You observe and write down specifics (including dates) for your employees'
   evaluations.
   Your staff evaluations show that you have observed your employees
   throughout the year.
   Your "plans of action" for employees needing improvement are reasonable and
   fair.
   You consistently encourage employee growth by providing accurate feedback
   on a regular basis for your employees.

ES   Your evaluations are not only unbiased, but perceptive, showing insight into the untapped abilities of the employee.
        Your "plans of action" are not only fair, but inventive, and consistently successful in improving employee performance.

NI   You document very few actions on your employees' evaluations.
        You wait until shortly before evaluations are due to document employees' actions.
        You are inconsistent in documenting observed actions for "exceeds standard."

9. **Actively coordinates with other departments.**

MS   You adjust your department's work flow to meet a library-wide need.
        You regularly attend and participate constructively at supervisors' meetings.
        You anticipate that a change in work flow might affect other departments and you coordinate as needed.

ES   You present a workable library-wide plan to improve overall service.

NI   You often put your own department's interests ahead of the library's service as a whole.
        You contribute little at supervisors' meetings.

APPENDIX C

Supervisory Procedures

Each supervisor receives the document Supervisory Procedures for Conducting a Performance Evaluation.

We have learned, through the turnover of two supervisory positions, that new supervisors (who were not involved in the initial discussions and revisions) need an individual review of what is expected.

The importance of the new supervisor's ongoing awareness and documentation of both "exceeds standard" and "needs improvement" behaviors and actions for his or her staff is emphasized during the new supervisor's orientation.

SUPERVISORY PROCEDURES FOR CONDUCTING A PERFORMANCE EVALUATION

- The supervisor meets with each employee of his or her staff by March 31 each year to exchange information about the employee's areas of strength and behaviors needing improvement, as applicable. The employee discusses what she or he needs from the supervisor to perform her or his job up to her or his potential.

- Additional performance meetings are held during the year with individual employees, as needed. All supervisors will hold an individual mid-year performance evaluation meeting with each member of his or her staff by July 31 each year.

- At each performance evaluation meeting, the supervisor and the employee discuss both strengths (with examples) and behaviors that need improvement (with examples), as applicable.

- When an employee has behaviors that need improvement, the supervisor and the employee agree upon an appropriate action plan.

- When there is a "needs improvement," there can be either a specific action plan for each standard or an overall action plan encompassing many of the standards.

- At the end of each performance evaluation meeting, the supervisor verifies that the employee understands what action is expected of him or her.

- By mid-October each year, the supervisor and employee meet to review the final evaluation for the year. At this point the employee has the opportunity to respond to the evaluation in written form within five (5) working days of the final appraisal.

- At the final meeting for the year, the supervisor indicates on the performance evaluation document his or her compensation recommendation for the employee.

- In order for an employee to receive an overall "meets standards" or "exceeds standards," the employee must have at least a 2.0 at point B2 on the tabulation sheet. This performance would reflect a level of at least "meets standards" for the employee's position responsibilities.

- An employee who begins employment at the library January 1 through June 30 is included in the current year's performance evaluation process.

- An employee who begins employment at the library July 1 through December 31 is included in the current year's performance evaluation process only if the supervisor determines the need to coach performance to reach an acceptable level.

- An employee who begins employment at the library July 1 through December 31 whose performance is at an acceptable level as determined by his or her supervisor will not receive a merit level increase but is eligible for a one-time performance bonus (prorated for actual employment time).

Performance Appraisal Document

The Performance Appraisal document is used by each supervisor to evaluate his or her staff. It is based upon the library's Code of Service.

For evaluation, the supervisor must document any pattern of continuing behavior which falls into the category of either "needs improvement" (NI) or "exceeds standard" (ES). If the employee "meets standard" (MS), the supervisor has the option of either documenting or not.

Evaluation of an employee is ongoing and is not based on single, unrelated actions.

PERFORMANCE APPRAISAL

NAME (last, first):   DATE:

POSITION:

SUPERVISOR:

BEGAN EMPLOYMENT:

The Standards of Performance system is based on the principle that an employee must know the expectations of the job and that the supervisor will inform the employee of how he or she is performing according to those expectations.

The supervisor will discuss this report with the employee and, if needed, will assist in developing an action plan for improvement.

In signing this report, the employee acknowledges having had the opportunity to review and discuss the performance appraisal, not necessarily that he or she is in agreement with the conclusions.

Upon completion and signature by employee and supervisor, this report is reviewed and signed by the Library Director.

Only the last three annual performance appraisals are kept active for review.

GUIDELINES FOR EVALUATION

- The Code of Service expresses the overall philosophy of service for the Library. The Code is the foundation upon which the Standards of Performance are built.

- The Standards of Performance are the types of behavior expected of an employee necessary to achieve the intent of the Code of Service.

- The Standards of Performance apply to daily performance. Throughout the year the supervisor regularly will evaluate, based on the Standards, the employee's performance.

- Effective evaluation is based on an employee's continuing pattern of behavior. Evaluation for any Standard of Performance is not based on single, unrelated actions.

- Evaluation of an employee is ongoing. When a supervisor perceives that an employee is having difficulty meeting a Standard of Performance, the supervisor is obligated to discuss with the employee what action is needed to meet the standard. The supervisor and the employee decide on the time and resources needed to meet the standard.

- For evaluation, the supervisor must document, with examples of specific, observed actions, any pattern of continuing behavior which either falls into the category of "needs improvement" (NI) or "exceeds standard" (ES). If an employee "meets standard" (MS), the supervisor has the option of either documenting or not.

- In order for an employee to receive an overall "meets standards" or "exceeds standards," the employee must have at least a 2.0 at point B2 on the tabulation sheet. This performance would reflect a level of at least "meets standards" for the employee's position responsibilities.

- Every employee's evaluation is reviewed by the Director, with the option of review by the Deputy Director.

- The employee's compensation is related directly to the employee's evaluation. The ove all pattern of the evaluation determines the employee's level of compensation.

- The employee always has both the right and the responsibility to discuss with his or her immediate supervisor any disparity between the employee's interpretation of his or her behavior and the supervisor's interpretation. If the employee and the supervisor cannot come to a mutually agreeable plan of action, the Director is the final arbiter.

PERFORMANCE STANDARDS

A. | **Service to Patrons and Coworkers**

1. *Makes eye contact, greets others sincerely, and speaks in a friendly manner.*

    Comments

    Examples of Behavior

    Action Plan

2. *Welcomes and serves without regard to race, color, religion, gender, sexual preference, national origin, disability, age, ancestry, or other characteristics.*

    Comments

    Examples of Behavior

    Action Plan

A.	**Service to Patrons and Coworkers** (continued)

3. *Acknowledges a patron's presence immediately, even if occupied.*

   Comments

   Examples of Behavior

   Action Plan

4. *Does not spend an undue amount of time or effort with one patron if another patron is waiting.*

   Comments

   Examples of Behavior

   Action Plan

5. *Takes personal responsibility for meeting patron and staff needs correctly (informational and physical access to materials).*

   Comments

   Examples of Behavior

   Action Plan

6. *Does not communicate any value judgment when interacting with a patron.*

   Comments

   Examples of Behavior

   Action Plan

A. **Service to Patrons and Coworkers** (continued)	
7. *Verifies with the patron or coworker that his or her needs have been met.*	
Comments	
Examples of Behavior	
Action Plan	
8. *Implements appropriate use of technology.*	
Comments	
Examples of Behavior	
Action Plan	

9. *Exhibits proper telephone use and etiquette.*

Comments

Examples of Behavior

Action Plan

10. *Exhibits a cooperative team spirit.*

Comments

Examples of Behavior

Action Plan

A. **Service to Patrons and Coworkers** (continued)	
11. *Puts service above any personal activities or interests while on duty.*	
Comments	
Examples of Behavior	
Action Plan	
12. *Is ready for duty at/during scheduled times.*	
Comments	
Examples of Behavior	
Action Plan	

13. *Is attentive to others' complaints and, when applicable, refers the complaints to the appropriate level.*

Comments

Examples of Behavior

Action Plan

14. *Takes responsibility for learning updated internal procedures.*

Comments

Examples of Behavior

Action Plan

A. **Service to Patrons and Coworkers** (continued)	
15. *Upholds library policies and established procedures.*	
Comments	
Examples of Behavior	
Action Plan	
16. *Upholds the intellectual freedom of the patron.*	
Comments	
Examples of Behavior	
Action Plan	

17. *Upholds all confidentiality rights of the patron.*

Comments

Examples of Behavior

Action Plan

B. **Personal Development**

1. *Plans own time to meet obligations and specified deadlines.*

   Comments

   Examples of Behavior

   Action Plan

2. *Actively listens to supervisor and accepts direction, seeking further advice from the supervisor as needed.*

   Comments

   Examples of Behavior

   Action Plan

3. *Accepts responsibility for own actions and obligations.*

Comments

Examples of Behavior

Action Plan

4. *Adapts to change.*

Comments

Examples of Behavior

Action Plan

B. **Personal Development** (continued)

5. *Uses library-provided means for continuing education or training.*

   Comments

   Examples of Behavior

   Action Plan

6. *Communicates clearly and honestly.*

   Comments

   Examples of Behavior

   Action Plan

7. *Demonstrates appropriate initiative within a team framework.*

Comments

Examples of Behavior

Action Plan

C. Specific Job Standards

Items under this category relate directly to the individual's position description.

C. **Specific Job Standards**

Items under this category relate directly to the individual's position description.

D. **Supervisory Standards**	
1. *Establishes cooperation and communication among staff.*	
Comments	
Examples of Behavior	
Action Plan	
2. *Makes appropriate decisions.*	
Comments	
Examples of Behavior	
Action Plan	

3. *Resolves problems fairly.*

Comments

Examples of Behavior

Action Plan

4. *Effectively and fairly manages the work flow of staff.*

Comments

Examples of Behavior

Action Plan

D. **Supervisory Standards** (continued)	
5. *Enforces all policies and work procedures fairly.*	
Comments	
Examples of Behavior	
Action Plan	
6. *Effectively and fairly manages resources.*	
Comments	
Examples of Behavior	
Action Plan	

7. *Works effectively with staff to improve performance.*

   Comments

   Examples of Behavior

   Action Plan

8. *Documents performance, then evaluates staff objectively and constructively, and in a timely manner.*

   Comments

   Examples of Behavior

   Action Plan

D. Supervisory Standards (continued)

9. *Actively coordinates with other departments.*

Comments

Examples of Behavior

Action Plan

Comments by Supervisor

Overall Action Plan

_____
Employee's signature   Date

_____
Supervisor's signature   Date

_____
Reviewer's signature   Date

Recommended for Level: _____

Comments by Employee

_____

Employee's signature   Date

_____

Supervisor's signature   Date

_____

Reviewer's signature   Date

APPENDIX E

Tabulation Sheet

Originally, the supervisors thought that the final "rating" for the employee's overall performance would be based on the feeling of how the final evaluation was weighted. For example, if the employee had many "meets," but just a few "exceeds," and no "needs improvement" standards, he or she would be a "meets standards" overall.

However, the supervisors' final decision to use a more precise (and obviously very objective) measurement resulted in the Standards of Performance Tabulation Sheet. This mathematical tabulation protects the objectivity of the final "rating" and assures the employee that his or her supervisor is evaluating the overall performance according to a set procedure—and not according to a subjective feeling.

STANDARDS OF PERFORMANCE
TABULATION SHEET

ES = 3 points; MS = 2 points; NI = 1 point
Round all numbers to the nearest "tenth" at each step of the calculation
(except B2)—Examples: 2.41 = 2.4 and 2.75 = 2.8.

1. Determine the total number of applicable standards for each:

   Service:_____
   Personal Development:_____

           Total above two categories: _____ **(A)**

   Specific Job Standards: _____
   Supervisory:_____

           Total above two categories: _____ **(B)**

2. Determine point value for each of the applicable sections:

   Service:
   number of ES X 3 = _____   number of MS X 2 =_____   number of NI =_____
           Total for Service Standards: _____

   Personal Development:
   number of ES X 3 = _____   number of MS X 2 =_____   number of NI =_____
           Total for Personal Development: _____

           Grand total of above two categories: _____ **(A1)**

   Specific Job Standards:
   number of ES X 3 = _____   number of MS X 2 =_____   number of NI =_____
           Total for Specific Job Standards: _____

   Supervisory:
   number of ES X 3 = _____   number of MS X 2 =_____   number of NI =_____
           Total for Supervisory Standards: _____

           Grand total of above two categories: _____ **(B1)**

STANDARDS OF PERFORMANCE
TABULATION SHEET

3. To determine the overall point value for Service and Development sections:

   Take **A1** _____ and divide by **A** _____

   This results in **A2:** _____ (the value for these sections)

4. To determine overall point value for the specific Job Standards and Supervisors:

   Take **B1** _____ and divide by **B** _____

   This results in **B2:** _____* (the value for these sections)

   > *** B2:**
   > **Must be 2.0 or higher to proceed with calculation.**

5. To determine overall point value for this evaluation:

   Add **A2** _____ to **B2** _____ This results in **B3:** _____

   Now divide **B3** by 2 _____ This is the total point value for this evaluation

   Using this number, the **overall evaluation** is rated _____

ES	= 2.5 or higher
MS3	= 2.4–2.2
MS2	= 2.1–1.8
MS1	= 1.7–1.5
NI	= 1.4 or lower

Employee's name: _____

Supervisor's signature:_____

Date: _____

INDEX

PATRICIA BELCASTRO currently is Deputy Director of Rocky River Public Library, Rocky River, Ohio. She has been both a children's librarian and an adult reference librarian, has worked in special libraries in both academic and business settings, and is a member of local, state, and national professional organizations. Most recently, she has focused on promoting readers' advisory service within the library and has written a successful grant for that purpose.